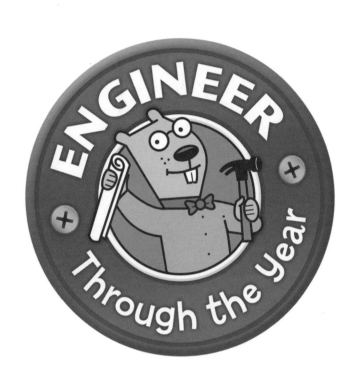

D1533085

Grades K-2

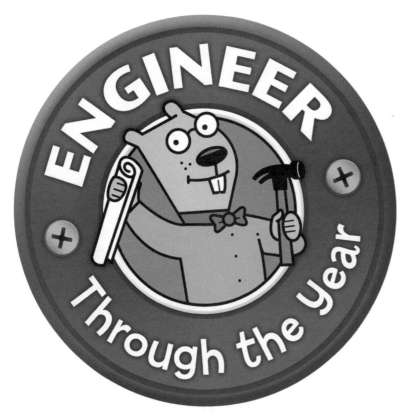

20 Turnkey STEM Projects
to Intrigue, Inspire & Challenge

Sandi Reyes

A division of Staff Development for Educators

Peterborough, New Hampshire

Published by Crystal Springs Books
A division of Staff Development for Educators (SDE)
10 Sharon Road, PO Box 500
Peterborough, NH 03458
1-800-321-0401
www.SDE.com/crystalsprings

© 2012 Sandi Reyes
Illustrations © 2012 Crystal Springs Books

Published 2012
Printed in the United States of America
16 15 14 13   2 3 4 5

ISBN: 978-1-935502-37-1
e-book ISBN: 978-1-935502-38-8

Library of Congress Cataloging-in-Publication Data

Reyes, Sandi, 1969-
Engineer through the year : 20 turnkey STEM projects to intrigue, inspire & challenge : grades
K-2 / Sandi Reyes.
   p. cm.
Includes bibliographical references.
ISBN 978-1-935502-37-1
1. Engineering--Study and teaching (Elementary)--United States. 2. Engineering--Study and
teaching (Elementary)--Activity programs. I. Title.

LB1594.R45 2012
372.35'8--dc23

                    2012008007

For Ariana and Maya...

Watching you grow and learn inspires me. May you grow up in a world
that supports creativity and innovative thinking.

Contents

Acknowledgments

For 15 years my husband, Gary, has had to share me with my classroom, an online business, and now this book. I would like to thank him for supporting me as I pursue my dreams, no matter where they take me or how much time they take.

I am forever grateful to the people who instilled in me the strengths I drew on while writing this book. My mother, Lenore, gave me a strong work ethic, attention to detail, and an obsessive need to achieve. Creativity and individuality were gifts from my father, Bob. And Aunt Barbara passed on a desire to teach children in a way that excites and engages, is developmentally appropriate, and creates lifelong learners.

All my love and thanks to Christy Miller for being a sounding board, a support system, a collaborator, and sometimes a "partner in crime." Her reminders to relax and to enjoy life have helped preserve my sanity throughout this process.

I need to thank Dawn Bean, Lynda Hammond, and Andrea Edwards for encouraging the growth of STEM in elementary schools, listening to my outlandish ideas, and helping me to make them happen. "Thanks" doesn't seem enough to express my appreciation to Judy Barbera for sharing her wisdom and for never letting me give up, no matter how hard I cried and begged.

Lastly, eternal gratitude goes out to Lisa Bingen for recognizing the need for this book and offering me the opportunity to write it. To Sharon Smith, thanks for guiding me every step of the way and demonstrating an enormous amount of patience with my naïveté about publishing. And to my editor, Marianne Knowles, thanks for understanding my vision and making this book amazing.

Dr. Seuss said, "Be who you are and say what you feel because those who mind don't matter and those who matter don't mind." I couldn't agree more.

Introduction

When I was asked to incorporate engineering education into my kindergarten classroom, I wondered how I could possibly squeeze any more into the school day, not to mention my workload. Then I compared what I was doing with my students to the requirements of engineering education and to STEM education in general. I was pleasantly surprised to find that much of what was already happening in my classroom—and probably in your classroom too—is exactly what STEM education is all about.

The best part was that I could take existing yearly themes and add an engineering challenge to each one, rather than rewriting the curriculum or adding yet another topic to the school day. By combining the science and math I was already teaching with a real-world design challenge, I was actually making less work for myself and better differentiated instruction for my students—all while giving them the benefits of STEM education and 21st Century Skills development.

What Is STEM? Why Is It Important?

STEM stands for Science, Technology, Engineering, and Mathematics. The essence of STEM is problem-based learning. Children are presented with a problem and design something that solves the problem. In the process, they activate science knowledge and math skills. They use technology to research, design, test, and present their ideas. As they work together, students learn and practice good collaboration and verbal communication—key skills identified by The Partnership for 21st Century Skills.

> "STEM jobs are the jobs of the future. They are essential for developing our technological innovation and global competitiveness."
>
> —from "STEM: Good Jobs Now and for the Future," U.S. Department of Commerce, Economics and Statistics Administration

What Does the Research Say?

Several studies have been conducted over the past 20 years regarding both STEM and project-based learning. Here are two of the most impressive.

"Open and Closed Mathematics":

Dr. Jo Boaler conducted an investigation into two schools in England that had similar students, but different approaches. After three years, students who followed a traditional approach developed a procedural knowledge that they had difficulty applying in unfamiliar situations. Students who learned mathematics in an open, project-based environment developed a conceptual understanding that allowed them significantly higher achievement in a range of assessments and situations.

—Boaler, "Open and Closed Mathematics"

How People Learn:

A few key points out of a wealth of research on how to best teach students: Students are more engaged and achieve better overall results when working in small collaborative groups on tasks that allow application of skills and processes. The more choice students have in their learning, the more they learn. And, the teacher who gradually releases responsibility to her students will see great results.

—Bransford, John D., et. al., *How People Learn*

1 Investigate

2 Brainstorm

3 Plan

4 Build

5 Test & Present

The Engineering Design Process

If you do any research, you'll find several different versions of the engineering design process. Most have been created to describe the general process followed by adults, then scaled back for use with children. The engineering design process used in this book, however, was designed for use in elementary schools. It intentionally follows a path similar to the one used to describe the scientific inquiry method. This was done to make the design process fit naturally into existing classroom practice; it is also developmentally appropriate for students to understand and use.

That being said, it is important to recognize that engineering design, like scientific inquiry, is messy. The engineering design diagram may show a perfect sequence, with one stage of the process leading neatly into the next, but this rarely happens in real life. Engineers, whether children or adults, bounce around, hitting each stage in an order that makes sense for a particular person and a particular design.

Regardless of the order in which they occur, certain behaviors are hallmarks of each stage of the process. The next several pages describe each stage of the process as it's used in this book.

Young Learners Are Natural Engineers

You may be thinking, "Engineering with young children? They can barely tie their shoes!" It may sound daunting, but it's really not difficult to do. From the time their hands can first grasp objects, children build. They put things together and take things apart. They may ask how things work, but they do not accept explanations—they investigate to find out for themselves. When faced with a challenge, children look to solve it without the restrictions that we adults place on ourselves. Nothing is impossible in a child's mind, and it is this kind of thinking that allows children to create ingenious inventions. It is what makes children such natural engineers.

This book offers step-by-step engineering activities that correlate to the most common yearlong themes taught in the primary grades. Two seasonal options are provided for each month of the school year. Each activity details every step of the challenge for seamless implementation into existing curriculum. The Content & Skills Alignment Charts on pages 163–166 show the integration of all 20 engineering challenges with the Next Generation Science Framework, 21st Century Skills as identified by The Partnership for 21st Century Skills, and the Common Core Standards for Mathematical Practice.

How to Use This Book

Each engineering design challenge activity is organized in the same easy-to-follow format. But don't let the structure mislead you. The challenges themselves are not a set of recipes or list of how-to instructions. They are open-ended experiences that require students to stretch themselves as they learn to generate ideas, solve problems, and work collaboratively with peers.

Challenge

Two seasonally appropriate Challenges are available for each month. Choose the Challenge that best meshes with your curricular themes and schedule.

Criteria for Product; Constraints for Challenge

The Criteria list clearly states for you and your students how to determine that a solution is successful. The Constraints specify limitations on time, materials, budget, or other resources.

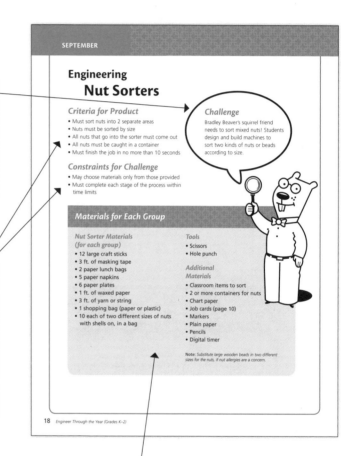

Materials

Quickly scan the Materials lists to determine which materials and tools you already have and which you may need to collect. Quantities are listed either per group or for the whole class, as noted. Any special or optional equipment for the Challenge is listed under Additional Materials.

Before You Begin

This handy list lets you know where in your curriculum the Challenge fits best, and provides directions for materials preparation and advance planning.

1 Investigate

During Investigate, students review relevant science and math concepts, explore examples of the objects they will design, examine the available materials, and review the Criteria for Product and Constraints for Challenge. Investigate contains one teacher-led activity; this provides students with a guided experience for materials exploration and research.

Before You Begin

- Prior to your class's first challenge, introduce students to the engineering design process and related definitions for engineering, criteria, constraints, and brainstorm.
- Prepare a materials kit for each group by placing the items from the nut sorter materials list into the shopping bag. Wind masking tape around a craft stick before placing it in the bag.
- Make a set of four job cards (page 10) for each group: Materials Manager, Timekeeper, Recorder, and Speaker.
- Make a copy of the Test Results (page 22) for each group.
- Make a copy of the Checklist (page 23) for each student.
- Set up the digital timer where students can check it.
- Write the Criteria for Product and Constraints for Challenge where students can see them.

Get Set

5-Step Process

1 Investigate *45 minutes*
- Demonstrate and discuss examples of sorting in real-world situations. Examples might include sorting clothes from the laundry or sorting eating utensils. Ask students to explain why people sort each kind of item.
- Provide opportunities for students to sort common classroom materials by a variety of characteristics.
- Show students the bag of mixed nuts. Tell them it will be their job to design and build a machine to sort the nuts by size. Give them a chance to examine the nuts. Ask students:
  Why might someone need to sort nuts?
  What are some different ways you could sort the nuts?
  What questions do you have about the challenge?
- Review with students the Criteria for Product and Constraints for Challenge, as well as the time limits for Brainstorm, Plan, and Build.

2 Brainstorm *20 minutes*
- Show students the items in a materials kit. Tell them they can use any of these materials to build their nut sorters. Ask students:
  What properties do these materials have?
  How can the properties of the materials help with a nut sorter?
- Review the meaning of *brainstorm*. Tell students that before they begin building, they need to come up with ideas.
- Give each student a piece of plain paper. Have students fold the paper in half vertically and again horizontally to make four boxes, then write "Brainstorm" along one edge of the page.

Engineer Through the Year (Grades K–2) 19

Helpful Classroom Technology

Use of current technology in the classroom both enhances teacher instruction and develops student skills. Note that using current technology is an enhancement; although the inclusion of such tools is recommended, students will be able to complete all design Challenges even if a recommended device is not available. The following items are suggested for use in some Challenges.

Teacher Use (Recommended)
- document camera
- projector or display monitor
- computer
- Internet access
- digital camera (still)
- digital camera (video)

Student Use (Optional)
- digital cameras (still)
- digital cameras (video)
- presentation software (for example, PowerPoint)
- word processing software

2 Brainstorm

During Brainstorm, students imagine what some solutions to the problem might look like. Students imagine, sketch, rearrange, and get ideas onto paper without stopping to analyze the merits of each. Grouping for Brainstorm varies—this stage may be completed alone, in small groups, or as a whole class, depending on the Challenge.

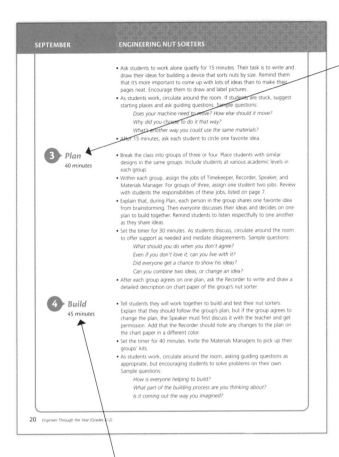

SEPTEMBER   ENGINEERING NUT SORTERS

- Ask students to work alone quietly for 15 minutes. Their task is to write and draw their ideas for building a device that sorts nuts by size. Remind them that it's more important to come up with lots of ideas than to make their pages neat. Encourage them to draw and label pictures.
- As students work, circulate around the room. If students are stuck, suggest starting places and ask guiding questions. Sample questions:
    Does your machine need to move? How else should it move?
    Why did you choose to do it that way?
    What's another way you could use the same materials?
- After 15 minutes, ask each student to circle one favorite idea.

3 ▸ Plan
40 minutes

- Break the class into groups of three or four. Place students with similar designs in the same groups. Include students at various academic levels in each group.
- Within each group, assign the jobs of Timekeeper, Recorder, Speaker, and Materials Manager. For groups of three, assign one student two jobs. Review with students the responsibilities of these jobs, listed on page 7.
- Explain that, during Plan, each person in the group shares one favorite idea from brainstorming. Then everyone discusses their ideas and decides on one plan to build together. Remind students to listen respectfully to one another as they share ideas.
- Set the timer for 30 minutes. As students discuss, circulate around the room to offer support as needed and mediate disagreements. Sample questions:
    What should you do when you don't agree?
    Even if you don't love it, can you live with it?
    Did everyone get a chance to show his ideas?
    Can you combine two ideas, or change an idea?
- After each group agrees on one plan, ask the Recorder to write and draw a detailed description on chart paper of the group's nut sorter.

4 ▸ Build
45 minutes

- Tell students they will work together to build and test their nut sorters. Explain that they should follow the group's plan, but if the group agrees to change the plan, the Speaker must first discuss it with the teacher and get permission. Add that the Recorder should note any changes to the plan on the chart paper in a different color.
- Set the timer for 40 minutes. Invite the Materials Managers to pick up their groups' kits.
- As students work, circulate around the room, asking guiding questions as appropriate, but encouraging students to solve problems on their own. Sample questions:
    How is everyone helping to build?
    What part of the building process are you thinking about?
    Is it coming out the way you imagined?

20   *Engineer Through the Year (Grades K–2)*

3 ▸ Plan

Students work in groups of three to four to develop the collaboration skills that rank high in importance in STEM and in 21st Century Skills education initiatives. Each student in a group chooses, or is assigned, one of four group jobs: Speaker, Timekeeper, Materials Manager, or Recorder; job assignments change with each challenge. During Plan, students share and evaluate the ideas generated during Brainstorm, then create one agreed-upon design.

The discussions that take place during Plan will reveal to you what your students know and how they think. It is during this time that connections to prior learning experiences take place, and that students are challenged to interpret the causes and effects of design decisions.

4 ▸ Build

Build is the most active phase of the engineering design process. Students put materials together and work cooperatively to build the objects they have designed. All students take part in building and in decision making, as well as performing the group jobs assigned during Plan. Students frequently test their solution during Build to determine whether it meets the Criteria for Product.

Students start Build by following their plan exactly, but challenges inevitably arise, especially during testing. Making changes to the original plan is a necessary part of the engineering design process. Just as important is the need for all group members to agree to the changes, and for the group to get approval for, and record, the changes being made.

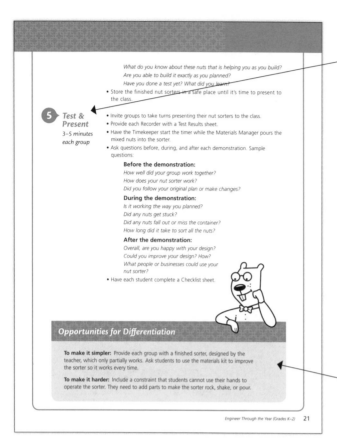

What do you know about these nuts that is helping you as you build?
Are you able to build it exactly as you planned?
Have you done a test yet? What did you learn?
• Store the finished nut sorters in a safe place until it's time to present to the class.

5 Test & Present
3–5 minutes each group

• Invite groups to take turns presenting their nut sorters to the class.
• Provide each Recorder with a Test Results sheet.
• Have the Timekeeper start the timer while the Materials Manager pours the mixed nuts into the sorter.
• Ask questions before, during, and after each demonstration. Sample questions:

Before the demonstration:
How well did your group work together?
How does your nut sorter work?
Did you follow your original plan or make changes?

During the demonstration:
Is it working the way you planned?
Did any nuts get stuck?
Did any nuts fall out or miss the container?
How long did it take to sort all the nuts?

After the demonstration:
Overall, are you happy with your design?
Could you improve your design? How?
What people or businesses could use your nut sorter?

• Have each student complete a Checklist sheet.

Opportunities for Differentiation

To make it simpler: Provide each group with a finished sorter, designed by the teacher, which only partially works. Ask students to use the materials kit to improve the sorter so it works every time.

To make it harder: Include a constraint that students cannot use their hands to operate the sorter. They need to add parts to make the sorter rock, shake, or pour.

Engineer Through the Year (Grades K–2) 21

5 Test & Present

In any real-world design task, engineers and scientists must present and demonstrate their work to an audience. The audience may include colleagues, investors, executives, politicians, the public, or consumers. Every design challenge offers an opportunity for students to present their solutions and test results to an audience. To mimic real-world presentations, a variety of audiences and presentation styles are suggested.

Opportunities for Differentiation

Options for making each design challenge simpler or harder let you adjust the classroom experience according to your students' grade level and prior experience with project-based learning, or to suit the time you have available to complete a project.

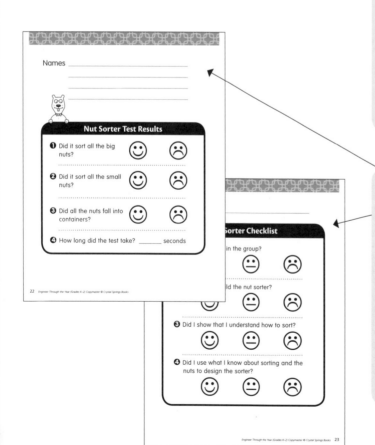

Test Results & Checklist

Challenge-specific Test Results pages give student groups a place to evaluate their product and record results. The Checklist helps individual students to reflect on their experience in engineering, and in functioning as part of a collaborative group. Both are provided as copymasters at the end of each engineering design challenge.

Moving Through the Year

Each challenge activity is set up in exactly the same format to create an easy-to-follow structure. Within this set structure, however, the directions for implementing each stage of the design process vary. The different strategies offered for each stage of a challenge give students the opportunity to practice different skills and to apply skills in new ways. The challenges offer a variety of ways to:

- guide student investigation
- support brainstorming
- group students
- choose student jobs for group work
- offer materials for building
- present results
- record observations and reflections

Strategies progress through the year from basic to complex, and from teacher-directed to student-directed. As the months pass, the design challenges release more responsibility to students as they become more capable of managing the design process on their own.

You're probably wondering if this means that you must start at the beginning of the year, do every challenge, and follow the guide exactly as it is written. Fortunately, the answer is "No." There are many ways to work with this guide and adjust it to the needs of your classroom.

Starting Midyear

If you begin to use this book in the middle of the year, or if you choose to do only a few activities throughout the year, then your students may not be ready for the suggested strategies for grouping or developing materials lists in a particular month. In this case, browse back to challenges in earlier months to find strategies that will work for your class. Think of it as a mix-and-match lesson plan design process. You may choose an activity based on its thematic connection to your current studies, but borrow strategies from other activities for different aspects of the design challenge.

Group Job Descriptions

Speakers make sure everyone gets a chance to talk. They also help solve disagreements, bring group questions to the teacher, arrange trades with other groups (when the challenge allows), and answer questions when the group presents their results.

Materials Managers get materials for the group. They also make any trades that the Speaker sets up, keep track of the budget if there is one, make sure that everyone in the group is using materials wisely, and test the product. Lastly, they organize cleanup by assigning tasks to each group member.

Timekeepers keep track of the time for each stage of the engineering design process. Timekeepers may assign different people to different tasks during Build so that everything gets done on time. They let the group know how much time is left, and help everyone stay on task so the work gets done before time runs out.

Recorders write down or draw all of the group's work, or direct others to do so when recording is a group effort. Recorders also keep track of any changes made to the design plan during Build, and record the results during Test & Present. Recorders take photos and videos of the group when cameras are used.

Page 10

Before beginning the challenges, make a set of four Job Cards for each group, working from the copymaster on page 10. Students use these cards to select jobs or to keep track of which job they have when jobs are assigned another way.

Adapting Challenges for Multiple Grades

Because this book is meant to work in a grade-level span, it is possible that teachers of different grade levels within a building will want to use the same challenges, resulting in second-grade students being presented with the same challenge they completed in kindergarten or first grade. If this happens, review the "make it harder" options under Opportunities for Differentiation. Other ways to make familiar challenges new include:

- If there is no budget limit included in the challenge, add one.

- Add a new length, width, height, volume, or weight requirement to the Criteria for Product.

- Think of something more that the object needs to do and add it to the Criteria for Product.

- Require the product to be visually attractive, if this is not part of the challenge.

- Require students to perform "market research" during Investigate. Have them gather information from potential "customers" to find out what they expect from the product.

- Make Present more challenging by adding specific technology requirements, such as the creation of brochures, newspaper ads, PowerPoint presentations, or spreadsheets.

A Word About Safety

The engineering design challenges in this book are safe for students in kindergarten through grade 2, but any activity carries some risk, however small. In general, the procedures you follow for safety during your regular science lessons also apply to engineering challenges. You can help further reduce the chance of mishaps by following a few common-sense guidelines.

- Be aware of food allergies among your students and substitute materials as needed.

- Any tool that has a sharp edge or that generates heat should be handled only by the teacher or an adult aide. (Examples: glue guns, pen knives, and awls)

- Check your state's guidelines before bringing materials from nature into the classroom.

- Use electrical appliances at least 3 feet away from any source of water. Avoid running electrical cords across pathways where students need to walk.

For further information, refer to the resource links on The National Science Teachers Association safety portal, www.nsta.org/portals/safety.

Planning Your Time

Another aspect of planning is figuring out how to fit all the stages of the engineering design process into your current daily schedule. There are natural places to stop each day as you work through a design challenge. Not all activities have the same time estimates for each stage of the process, but the chart below offers a basic look at how the process divides up.

Before the Challenge	Time needed to complete the preparation listed in **Before You Begin** varies depending on the challenge.
Day 1	The **Investigate** stage can usually be completed in one day.
Day 2	The **Brainstorm** and **Plan** stages can usually be completed together, with careful attention to time management and minimal issues with transition.
Days 3 & 4	**Build** will take at least one session, but plan on two or more, depending on time estimates provided for the design challenge.
Day 5	**Test & Present** takes 5–10 minutes per group and typically can be completed in one session. More involved presentations that require special testing setups or creating digital media may take two sessions.

This chart assumes a one-hour session per day. Plan for additional days if your sessions are less than one hour.

Regardless of whether it is the beginning of the year, the end of the year, or anywhere in between, you can introduce your students to engineering. Choose a challenge that supports where you are in your current curriculum and get started!

Job Cards

Materials Manager

Recorder

Speaker

Timekeeper

Engineer Through the Year (Grades K-2) Copymaster © Crystal Springs Books

Engineering
Apple Containers

Criteria for Product

- Must be easy to carry
- Must have handles of some kind
- Must be large enough to hold at least three apples
- Must hold the apples without anyone's hands under it
- Apples must stay in container while it is carried 10 steps

Constraints for Challenge

- May choose materials only from the ones provided
- Must complete each stage in the time allowed

Challenge

It's harvest time! Students design and build easy-to-carry containers to hold as many apples as possible.

Materials

Apple Container Materials (for class)

- 10+ apples, various sizes
- 1 roll of aluminum foil
- 1 roll of waxed paper
- 16+ foam trays
- 100 assorted index cards
- 50 paper plates
- 1 box of craft sticks (about 300)
- 100 sheets of paper
- 1 box of sandwich bags
- 50 straws
- 1 box of paper clips
- 2 rolls of clear tape
- 1 roll of yarn or string

Tools

- Scissors
- Hole punch

Additional Materials

- Chart paper
- Job card sets
- Markers
- Plain paper
- Pencils
- Digital timer
- Digital video camera (optional)

Before You Begin

- Prior to your class's first challenge, introduce students to the engineering design process and related definitions for engineering, criteria, constraints, and brainstorm.
- Set the apple container materials out on a table.
- Make a copy of the Test Results (page 16) for each group.
- Make a copy of the Checklist (page 17) for each student.
- Make a set of four job cards (page 10) for each group: Materials Manager, Timekeeper, Recorder, and Speaker.
- Set up the digital timer where students can check on it.
- Display the Criteria and Constraints where students can see them.

5-Step Process

1 Investigate
45 minutes

- Pass around some apples and give students a few minutes to explore their sizes and shapes.
- Tell students they have a problem to solve. It's harvest time, and workers are busy picking apples. The apples must be moved to the other side of the orchard. The challenge is to design a container to carry as many apples as possible. Ask students:

    What properties of apples do you need to consider when you design? (for example, size, shape, weight)

    What are some different ways that you carry items?

    Do apples stack neatly?

    What questions do you have about the challenge?

- Review with students the Criteria for Product and Constraints for Challenge. Also review the time limits for Brainstorm, Plan, and Build.

2 Brainstorm
30 minutes

- Show students the items on the materials table. Tell them that they will have these materials to work with. They can use any of these materials—but no others—to build their apple containers.
- Invite a few students at a time to come examine the materials. Ask students:

    What properties do these materials have?

    How can the properties of the materials help an apple container to work?

- Review the meaning of brainstorm. Tell students that before they begin building, they need to come up with ideas.
- Give each student a piece of plain paper. Have students fold the paper in half vertically and again horizontally to make four boxes, then write "Brainstorm" along one edge of the page (or do this for them as needed).
- Ask students to work alone quietly for 15 minutes. Their task is to think of

four different ideas for building an apple container, using the materials they just looked at. Students draw a different idea in each of the four boxes. If a student has more than four ideas, suggest using the other side of the paper.

- As students work, walk around the room and ask guiding questions to extend student thinking. Suggest starting places for those who are stuck. Sample questions:

    How would you carry your apple container?

    Why did you choose that material instead of another?

    How does your container keep the apples from rolling out?

    How many apples do you think that container might carry?

    Which design is your favorite? Why?

- After 15 minutes, ask each student to choose one favorite idea and circle it. Explain that they will get into groups. Their group will come up with one design to build. It might be like their favorite design, or it might be different.

3 ▶ Plan

40 minutes

- Think of your class in terms of four levels of academic ability. Then create mixed-ability groups of three to four students each. Have students sit with their groups.

- Explain that all group members help plan and build the container. But each group member also has one of four special jobs.

    - Speakers make sure everyone gets a chance to talk. They also bring questions to the teacher, help solve disagreements before asking the teacher to help, and answer questions when the group presents.

    - Timekeepers keep track of the time. To make sure everything gets done on time, they assign different tasks to different group members and help keep everyone on task.

    - Materials Managers get materials for the group and test the container. They are also in charge of organizing cleanup.

    - Recorders write down or draw all of the group's work, including the plan and the test results.

- Place a set of job cards upside down on each table. Have each student choose one job card. (For groups with three students, one student takes two jobs.) Tell students that they may not trade jobs or groups, but they will do different jobs on other challenges.

- Set the timer for 30 minutes for groups to Plan. Have students explain their ideas to each other and then decide on one idea to build. Remind students that each person needs to share before the group decides. Make sure they understand that they may also combine ideas, or change an idea to make it better.

- Circulate around the room to offer support as needed and to mediate disagreements. Sample questions:

    Did you choose one person's idea, or combine several ideas?

    How can you disagree with someone and still be respectful?

How are you all showing that you can listen actively?

How did you go about sharing ideas? Did you talk about one idea at a time, or more than one idea? Did you talk about ways to make an idea work better?

• After each group agrees, provide a piece of chart paper. Ask the Recorder to draw and label a diagram of the group's apple container and include a list of the materials their plan calls for, with approximate amounts.

4 Build

45 minutes

• Tell students they will now work in groups to build and test their apple containers. Set the timer for 45 minutes.

• Materials Managers collect the materials from the group's list.

• Remind students to begin by following their plans. If a group wants to change their plans, they may. First, the whole group must agree to make the change. Then, the Speaker must get permission from the teacher. The Recorder then uses a different color marker to record any changes to the plan.

• As students work, circulate around the room. Ask guiding questions as appropriate, but encourage students to solve problems on their own. Sample questions:

What part of the build is each person working on?

Is the container coming out the way you imagined?

What do you know about apples that you are thinking about as you build?

How will you carry the container?

Have you done a test yet?

Did you change your container after a test? If so, then why?

• Place the finished apple containers in a safe place until students are ready to present to the class.

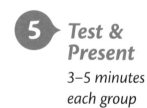

5 Test & Present

3–5 minutes each group

• Invite each group to take a turn presenting the apple container to the class.

• Provide each Recorder with a Test Results sheet for recording results. Consider recording each presentation using a digital video camera.

• Have the Materials Manager place three apples in the container, pick it up, and carry it for 10 regular-size steps.

• If the apples remain in the container, the Timekeeper adds one more apple. The Materials Manager carries the container back for another 10 regular-size steps. Each group continues until their container fails.

• Ask questions before, during, and after each demonstration. Sample questions:

Before the demonstration:

How does your apple container work?

Did you follow your original plan or did you make changes?

Why did you make those changes?

Give one example of how your group used cooperation.

During the demonstration:

Is it working the way you planned?

How many apples did your container carry? (The apple that broke the container doesn't count.)

When the container failed, did the container break or did the apples fall out?

Did the container show signs of wear before it broke?

After the demonstration:

Do you think your design was successful? Why?

What part of your design could you improve?

What people or businesses could use your apple container?

• Have each student complete a Checklist sheet.

Opportunities for Differentiation

To make it simpler: Provide each group with an identical pre-made container. Before you begin, cut, fold, and tape a piece of paper into a basic container that is large enough to hold three apples but not strong enough to support their weight. Instruct the groups to use the materials to improve this container so that it meets all of the Criteria for Product.

To make it harder: Instruct students to design a container that can be carried with only one hand or over a shoulder.

Names _____

_____

_____

_____

Apple Container Test Results

❶ Is it easy to carry?

❷ Does it have handles?

❸ Did 3 apples stay in for 10 steps?

❹ How many apples did the container hold? _____ apples

Name _____

Apple Container Checklist

❶ Did I do my job in the group?

❷ Did I share my ideas?

❸ Did I listen to others' ideas?

❹ Did I help build the apple container?

❺ Did I use what I know about apples and about the materials to make my design?

Engineering
Nut Sorters

Criteria for Product

- Must sort nuts into 2 separate areas
- Nuts must be sorted by size
- All nuts that go into the sorter must come out
- All nuts must be caught in a container
- Must finish the job in no more than 10 seconds

Constraints for Challenge

- May choose materials only from those provided
- Must complete each stage of the process within time limits

Challenge

Bradley Beaver's squirrel friend needs to sort mixed nuts! Students design and build machines to sort two kinds of nuts or beads according to size.

Materials for Each Group

Nut Sorter Materials (for each group)

- 12 large craft sticks
- 3 ft. of masking tape
- 2 paper lunch bags
- 5 paper napkins
- 6 paper plates
- 1 ft. of waxed paper
- 3 ft. of yarn or string
- 1 shopping bag (paper or plastic)
- 10 each of two different sizes of nuts with shells on, in a bag

Tools

- Scissors
- Hole punch

Additional Materials

- Classroom items to sort
- 2 or more containers for nuts
- Chart paper
- Job cards (page 10)
- Markers
- Plain paper
- Pencils
- Digital timer

Note: *Substitute large wooden beads in two different sizes for the nuts, if nut allergies are a concern.*

Before You Begin

- Prior to your class's first challenge, introduce students to the engineering design process and related definitions for engineering, criteria, constraints, and brainstorm.
- Prepare a materials kit for each group by placing the items from the nut sorter materials list into the shopping bag. Wind masking tape around a craft stick before placing it in the bag.
- Make a set of four job cards (page 10) for each group: Materials Manager, Timekeeper, Recorder, and Speaker.
- Make a copy of the Test Results (page 22) for each group.
- Make a copy of the Checklist (page 23) for each student.
- Set up the digital timer where students can check it.
- Write the Criteria for Product and Constraints for Challenge where students can see them.

5-Step Process

1 Investigate
45 minutes

- Demonstrate and discuss examples of sorting in real-world situations. Examples might include sorting clothes from the laundry or sorting eating utensils. Ask students to explain why people sort each kind of item.
- Provide opportunities for students to sort common classroom materials by a variety of characteristics.
- Show students the bag of mixed nuts. Tell them it will be their job to design and build a machine to sort the nuts by size. Give them a chance to examine the nuts. Ask students:

  Why might someone need to sort nuts?

  What are some different ways you could sort the nuts?

  What questions do you have about the challenge?

- Review with students the Criteria for Product and Constraints for Challenge, as well as the time limits for Brainstorm, Plan, and Build.

2 Brainstorm
20 minutes

- Show students the items in a materials kit. Tell them they can use any of these materials to build their nut sorters. Ask students:

  What properties do these materials have?

  How can the properties of the materials help with a nut sorter?

- Review the meaning of *brainstorm*. Tell students that before they begin building, they need to come up with ideas.
- Give each student a piece of plain paper. Have students fold the paper in half vertically and again horizontally to make four boxes, then write "Brainstorm" along one edge of the page.

- Ask students to work alone quietly for 15 minutes. Their task is to write and draw their ideas for building a device that sorts nuts by size. Remind them that it's more important to come up with lots of ideas than to make their pages neat. Encourage them to draw and label pictures.
- As students work, circulate around the room. If students are stuck, suggest starting places and ask guiding questions. Sample questions:

    Does your machine need to move? How else should it move?

    Why did you choose to do it that way?

    What's another way you could use the same materials?

- After 15 minutes, ask each student to circle one favorite idea.

3 ▶ Plan
40 minutes

- Break the class into groups of three or four. Place students with similar designs in the same groups. Include students at various academic levels in each group.
- Within each group, assign the jobs of Timekeeper, Recorder, Speaker, and Materials Manager. For groups of three, assign one student two jobs. Review with students the responsibilities of these jobs, listed on page 7.
- Explain that, during Plan, each person in the group shares one favorite idea from brainstorming. Then everyone discusses their ideas and decides on one plan to build together. Remind students to listen respectfully to one another as they share ideas.
- Set the timer for 30 minutes. As students discuss, circulate around the room to offer support as needed and mediate disagreements. Sample questions:

    What should you do when you don't agree?

    Even if you don't love it, can you live with it?

    Did everyone get a chance to show his ideas?

    Can you combine two ideas, or change an idea?

- After each group agrees on one plan, ask the Recorder to write and draw a detailed description on chart paper of the group's nut sorter.

4 ▶ Build
45 minutes

- Tell students they will work together to build and test their nut sorters. Explain that they should follow the group's plan, but if the group agrees to change the plan, the Speaker must first discuss it with the teacher and get permission. Add that the Recorder should note any changes to the plan on the chart paper in a different color.
- Set the timer for 40 minutes. Invite the Materials Managers to pick up their groups' kits.
- As students work, circulate around the room, asking guiding questions as appropriate, but encouraging students to solve problems on their own. Sample questions:

    How is everyone helping to build?

    What part of the building process are you thinking about?

    Is it coming out the way you imagined?

What do you know about these nuts that is helping you as you build?

Are you able to build it exactly as you planned?

Have you done a test yet? What did you learn?

- Store the finished nut sorters in a safe place until it's time to present to the class.

5 Test & Present

3–5 minutes each group

- Invite groups to take turns presenting their nut sorters to the class.
- Provide each Recorder with a Test Results sheet.
- Have the Timekeeper start the timer while the Materials Manager pours the mixed nuts into the sorter.
- Ask questions before, during, and after each demonstration. Sample questions:

Before the demonstration:

How well did your group work together?

How does your nut sorter work?

Did you follow your original plan or make changes?

During the demonstration:

Is it working the way you planned?

Did any nuts get stuck?

Did any nuts fall out or miss the container?

How long did it take to sort all the nuts?

After the demonstration:

Overall, are you happy with your design?

Could you improve your design? How?

What people or businesses could use your nut sorter?

- Have each student complete a Checklist sheet.

Opportunities for Differentiation

To make it simpler: Provide each group with a finished sorter, designed by the teacher, which only partially works. Ask students to use the materials kit to improve the sorter so it works every time.

To make it harder: Include a constraint that students cannot use their hands to operate the sorter. They need to add parts to make the sorter rock, shake, or pour.

Names _____

_____

_____

_____

Nut Sorter Test Results

❶ Did it sort all the big nuts?

❷ Did it sort all the small nuts?

❸ Did all the nuts fall into containers?

❹ How long did the test take? _____ seconds

Name _____

Nut Sorter Checklist

❶ Did I do my job in the group?

❷ Did I help to build the nut sorter?

❸ Did I show that I understand how to sort?

❹ Did I use what I know about sorting and the nuts to design the sorter?

Engineering
Columbus Day Sailboats

Criteria for Product

- Must sail across a tub of water
- Must be powered by the wind from an electric fan
- Must carry at least five weights
- Must float for the whole trip

Constraints for Challenge

- May use only materials provided in the kit
- Must complete each stage in the time allowed
- Fan must stay on the same speed for each test
- Fan cannot be tilted or moved during the test

Challenge

Christopher Columbus needs to sail across the ocean. Students design and build sailboats that float across the water powered only by wind.

Materials

Sailboat Materials (for each group)

- 2 foam trays
- 2 ft. of aluminum foil
- 2 ft. of waxed paper
- 1 sheet of felt, any color
- 2 paper lunch bags
- 1 sheet of tissue paper
- 5 sheets of paper (plain or construction)
- 6 coffee stirrers
- 6 craft sticks
- 3 paper plates
- 3 small paper drink cups
- 1 roll of clear tape
- 2 plastic shopping bags

Tools

- Tape measure
- Hole punch
- Scissors

Additional Materials

- 5 or more bolts or large washers for each group (to use as weights)
- Chart paper
- Electric fan (a box fan works best)
- Computer with projector
- Markers
- Plain paper
- Pencils
- Job cards (page 10)
- Digital timer
- Towels (to mop up spills)
- Long, shallow tub to hold water (35+ in. long x 7+ in. deep)
- Digital video cameras (optional)

Before You Begin

- Prepare a materials kit for each group. Place all of the materials on the Sailboat Materials list into a shopping bag. Set out additional kit materials for the Investigate stage.
- Search online for examples of sail design through history. Helpful search terms include "sailboat," "pirate ship," and "ancient sailboat."
- Make a copy of the Test Results (page 29) for each group.
- Make a copy of the Checklist (page 30) for each student.
- Make a set of job cards (page 10) for each group.
- Display the Criteria for Product and Constraints for Challenge where students can see them.
- Set up the digital timer where students can check it.
- Fill the tub with water, leaving about 2 inches at the top.
- Set up the fan where it can blow across the tub, but where there is no risk of water contacting electric current.

5-Step Process

1 ▸ Investigate
2 sessions of 45 minutes each

- Students need familiarity with the properties of materials before they can design their sailboats. During the first session, give students a chance to test the materials in the tub of water to determine which sink and which float. Ask students:

    Which materials are waterproof? Which are not?

    Does a material have to be waterproof to float?

    Does a material sink if it's one shape, but float if it's another?

    Are there combinations of materials that float better together?

    Encourage students to think up their own tests to try on the materials.

- During the second session, provide opportunities for students to hold different materials in the wind from the fan and observe how each material acts. Ask students:

    How does the material move in the wind?

    Which materials catch more wind than others?

    Does it make a difference how thick or thin a material is?

- Show students the images of historical sail designs that you found. Explain to students that when Christopher Columbus wanted to cross the ocean, he used the best technology available to him: sailboats. Sailboats are a very old technology, but like most technology, they take a lot of planning and testing to build.

- Tell students that they will design sailboats in honor of Columbus. Read the Criteria for Product and Constraints for Challenge and explain anything that isn't clear. Point out the time limits for the Brainstorm, Plan, and Build stages.

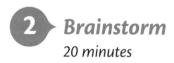

2 ▶ Brainstorm
20 minutes

- Show students the materials kit. Tell them they may plan to use any materials in the kit—but no other items—to build their sailboats.
- Set out samples of each material in the kit so students can touch and examine the samples while brainstorming.
- Give each student a sheet of plain paper. Have them write Brainstorm at the top.
- Instruct students to work silently and independently for 15 minutes. Tell them to think of as many different designs for a sailboat as possible. Explain that they may think of using different materials for each design, or they may use the same materials in different ways.
- Encourage students to label diagrams with the parts *sail* and *boat* and with the materials to be used (for example, *tissue, foil*).
- While students brainstorm, walk around the room. Ask guiding questions to encourage detailed work and offer starting places for students who are stuck. Suggested questions:

  How do you know that your boat will float?

  What shapes could you use for the boat?

  Will you use one sail or more than one sail in your design?

  What shapes could you use for a sail? How big will it be?

  What properties of sails do you need to think about when you design?

  Does the material you use affect how well a sail works?

  What do you know about air that can help you design a sail?

  What questions do you have about the challenge?

- After 15 minutes, ask each student to choose one favorite idea and circle it.
- Collect all brainstorming papers.

3 ▶ Plan
30 minutes

- Before Plan begins, review the "favorite idea" designs on all Brainstorm papers, then make groups of three to four students, placing students with similar designs together. Design similarities could be number of sails, sail shape, or sail material.
- Return the Brainstorm papers to students by group. Give each group a set of job cards. Instruct each group to turn the job cards face down on the table. Then each student chooses a job card: Speaker, Materials Manager, Timekeeper, or Recorder. (For groups of three, one student chooses two jobs.) Students may not trade jobs. Review the responsibilities of the four group jobs (page 7). Remind students that each group member helps build, in addition to doing a job.
- Set the timer for 20 minutes. Instruct students to review their favorite designs with others in their group, looking for similarities. Encourage groups to use similarities as a starting place for a group plan. Remind them that after all members have shared, the group comes up with one plan that they all think will work.

- As students discuss, circulate around the room to offer support as needed and mediate disagreements. Sample questions:

  How are your four favorite designs alike?

  Did you choose one person's design or did you use pieces of many designs?

  How is your final design like your four favorite designs? How is it different?

  How will you hold up your sail?

- After each group agrees on one plan, the Recorder leads the group in writing the plan on chart paper. The plan needs a diagram and labels. Each material should be drawn in a different color so that the diagram is easy to understand (for example, aluminum foil drawn in red, waxed paper drawn in green).

4 Build
60 minutes

- Review with students the procedure for Build. Start by following the group's plan. However, as they build, they may realize that they need to make changes. When that happens, the Speaker must notify the teacher. Then the Recorder makes changes to the plan in a different color or creates a Plan 2 on a different chart.

- Tell students they will work as a group to build and test their sailboats. Set the timer for 50 minutes and invite each Materials Manager to pick up a materials kit and five weights for testing.

- As needed, remind Timekeepers to watch how much time is left, make sure the group makes progress, and participate in the construction of the sailboat. Check in with students doing other jobs, as well.

- Encourage students to test their boats from time to time, then make changes as needed.

- As students work, monitor the progress of each group. Remind students to use teamwork and cooperation. Sample questions to ask while monitoring:

  What part of the sailboat are you building now?

  How are you settling disagreements?

  Is the design coming out the way you thought it would?

  What do you know about air and water that you are considering as you build?

  Why did you choose that material?

  Have you made any changes to your plan?

  Have you tested to see if your boat holds five weights?

  Have you tested your sail(s)? What did you learn?

- When a sailboat is ready for its final test, the Speaker should notify the teacher. If you are having groups make videos of the tests, then test each sailboat as each group finishes. If groups are presenting tests live, then set aside the sailboats until it is time to test.

5 **Test & Present**

5–10 minutes each group

- The testing procedure applies whether or not you are making videos.
- The Recorder captures the test on a video camera (optional).
- The Speaker narrates the test, explaining what is happening.
- The Materials Manager adds five weights to the boat and places the boat in the water.
- The Timekeeper turns on the fan and measures how far the boat sails in 30 seconds.
- If the boat makes it completely across the water, the Materials Manager adds one more weight to the boat and tests again. Each time the boat is successful, another weight is added. When the boat fails, the test is over.
- The Recorder completes the Test Results sheet.
- Time permitting, students may work on an improved sailboat design after their formal test.
- Encourage the class to ask questions during the presentations and have the Speaker answer their questions.
- Have each student complete a Checklist sheet.

Opportunities for Differentiation

To make it simpler: Make boat bottoms in advance for each group. Cut a slit in the center of a foam food tray and add a craft stick as the mast. Have students create only one sail for the boat.

To make it harder: Increase the weight the boat is required to carry. Require the boat to move across the tub in a certain amount of time.

Names _____

_____

_____

_____

Columbus Day Sailboat Test Results

❶ Did your boat sail all the way across the tub?   Yes   No

❷ Did your boat hold 5 weights?   Yes   No

❸ Did your boat float for the whole trip?   Yes   No

❹ How many weights did your boat hold?   _____ weights

❺ How long did it take your boat to cross the tub?   _____ seconds

Name _____

Columbus Day Sailboat Checklist

❶ Was I a good member of my group?

      Yes   Sort of   No

❷ Did I help to build the sailboat?

      Yes   Sort of   No

❸ Did I try a new design if I needed to?

      Yes   No

❹ Did I use what I know about air and water in my design?

      Yes   Sort of   No

❺ Did I choose materials that had good properties for the boat and the sail?

      Yes   Sort of   No

Engineering
Pumpkin Packages

Criteria for Product

- Pumpkin must go in and come out without damage to package or pumpkin
- Must be easy to put the pumpkin in the package and take it out again
- Package must keep pumpkin safe (no cracks, dents, or bruises) when dropped from 10 feet or higher
- Pumpkin must stay in the package when dropped
- Package must include four or more different materials

Constraints for Challenge

- May choose materials only from those provided
- Must complete each stage in the time allowed

Challenge

Fall is time for pumpkins! These giant fruits are fragile. Students design and construct packages to keep pumpkins safe when dropped.

Materials

Pumpkin Package Materials (for class)

- Shopping bags
- Resealable sandwich bags
- Paper lunch bags
- Foam plates and trays
- Paper towel and bath tissue tubes
- Paper
- Balloons (assorted)
- Newspapers
- Packing materials
- Paper towels or napkins
- Craft sticks
- Straws
- Masking tape
- Yarn or string

Note: *Provide materials or suitable substitutes in whatever quantities are readily available.*

Tools

- Balloon or ball pump
- Scissors
- Staplers
- Hole punch
- Tape measure

Additional Materials

- Examples of packaging
- Job cards (page 10)
- Chart paper
- Markers
- Plain paper
- Pencils
- Digital timer
- A few pumpkins in various sizes
- 1 pumpkin per group of the same size and weight
- Digital video camera (optional)

Before You Begin

- For the Investigate stage, collect packaging examples such as boxes, bubble wrap, plastic blister packs, foam inserts, padded envelopes, CD cases, and so forth.
- Review the materials list, make substitutions, gather materials, and shop for pumpkins.
- Encourage families to send in packaging examples and materials for building pumpkin packages.
- Scout out a location for testing, as described under Test & Present.
- Recruit one or more additional adults to assist during testing.
- Make a copy of Test Results (page 36) for each group.
- Make a copy of Checklist (page 37) for each student.
- Make a set of job cards (page 10) for each group.
- Set the pumpkin package materials out on a table.
- Write the numbers 1, 2, 3, and 4 on separate slips of paper so that each group has a set of numbers 1 to 4.
- Set up the digital timer where students can check it.
- Display the Criteria for Product and Constraints for Challenge where students can see them.

5-Step Process

 Investigate
60 minutes

- Ask students to imagine that they need to send something large to a friend or relative who lives far away. How would they send it? Would they just stick stamps on it and put it in a mailbox? Why or why not?
- Pass around some examples of packaging. Ask students what these materials are used for. What might happen to products if the package were not there? Guide students to recognize that, without packaging, products might be damaged during shipping. Explain that some engineers specialize in designing packages to protect products during shipping.
- Bring out a variety of pumpkins. Tell students that they'll be designing a package that can safely ship a pumpkin. Shipping can be rough on a product—packages sometimes get dropped, even when package carriers are careful. If the package helps protect the pumpkin when it is dropped, then it will probably survive whatever else happens to it.
- Tell students that, before they can design a package, they have to know something about the product they're shipping. Give students a chance to explore the properties of pumpkins. Encourage students to investigate a pumpkin's shape, weight, circumference (how big around it is), diameter (how big across it is), and how easily it rolls. Ask students:

  What pumpkin properties should you think about when designing a package?

  Do you think a pumpkin would break easily? Would it bruise?

How do pumpkins move? Do they roll? Slide? How can you keep them from moving around inside a package?

Do you have any questions about the challenge?

- Review with students the Criteria for Product and Constraints for Challenge, as well as the time limits for Brainstorm, Plan, and Build.

② Brainstorm
30 minutes

- Set out pumpkins that are all about the same size and weight. Tell students that each group will package one of these pumpkins.
- Show students the items on the materials table. Explain that each pumpkin package must use at least four different materials from the table. Call small groups up to the table to examine and touch the materials. Ask students:

  What properties do these materials have?

  How can the properties of the materials help?

  How could each of these materials be used in the design?

- Give each student a piece of paper. Have them fold the paper in half vertically and again horizontally to make four boxes, and write "Brainstorm" along one edge.
- Have students work alone for 15 minutes to draw diagrams of four different pumpkin packages, one diagram in each square of the folded paper.
- Support and extend student thinking by visiting students to ask questions such as the following.

  Did you use four or more materials in this design?

  How does that design open and close so you can put the pumpkin in and take it out?

  Which materials keep the pumpkin safe when it falls?

- After 15 minutes, ask each student to choose one favorite idea and circle it.

③ Plan
30 minutes

- Consider the learning modalities among your students—for example, whether each is a kinesthetic, visual, or auditory learner, or shows another strong learning preference.
- Create groups of three to four students so that each group has different learning styles mixed together. Do not consider academic levels for this challenge.
- Provide each group a set of paper slips numbered 1 to 4 and a set of job cards. Have students within each group choose a numbered slip at random and then choose job cards in order, 1 to 4. (For groups of three, have one student take two jobs.) Review the responsibilities of the four jobs: Speaker, Materials Manager, Timekeeper, and Recorder (page 7). Remind students that they may not trade jobs, but each will do a different job on another challenge.
- Set the timer for 20 minutes. Instruct students to take turns sharing their favorite Brainstorm idea, following the same 1 to 4 order. After all members have shared, the group draws up one plan that they all think will work. Encourage groups to jot down ideas on fresh paper as they talk.

- As students discuss, circulate to offer support and mediate any disagreements that the Speakers cannot resolve. Sample questions:

  What is it about this plan that you all like?

  Is each person involved in decision making? Explain each person's part to me.

  How does your design show that you understand the properties of a pumpkin?

  Is anything in your plan not part of the criteria? Why did you include it?

- As each group agrees on a plan, provide chart paper and markers. The Recorder assigns each person in the group part of the plan to write or draw on the chart paper. Each plan needs a diagram, labels, and a materials list. The materials list needs at least four materials and cannot have any material that is not on the table.

Build
60 minutes

- Tell students they will work as a group to build and test their pumpkin packages. Set the timer for 60 minutes. Invite Materials Managers to gather the items listed in their group's plan, as well as one pumpkin. Tell any group that plans to use balloons that, for safety reasons, they must borrow the pump to inflate the balloons—they must not use their mouths. (You may prefer to inflate and tie balloons yourself.)

- Remind students to follow their plan as they build. A plan may change only if all students in the group agree. Then the Speaker gets permission from the teacher and the Recorder makes changes to the plan using a different color, or draws it as Plan 2 on a new chart.

- As students work, walk around the room, conferencing with each group and encouraging students to solve problems on their own. Sample questions:

  How is each person helping?

  Is your group using good teamwork skills?

  Are all the materials working the way you planned?

  Have you made any changes to your plans?

  How will your package keep your pumpkin safe?

  Are you measuring as you go to be sure that the pumpkin will fit?

- Remind students that everyone in the group helps build, in addition to doing their assigned jobs.

Test & Present
5–10 minutes per group

- Locate a testing area (outdoors if possible) where the pumpkin package can be dropped from a height of at least 10 feet. Good options include dropping the package out of a second story window or from the top of bleachers or a jungle gym. The test will be more challenging if there is a hard surface below.

- Confirm that your adult helpers can attend, so that there is at least one adult at the top and one at the bottom of the drop site.

- Decide how to manage testing. One option is to gather the class as a group. Another is to test each group's package as they finish and record each test with a digital video camera. Then present and discuss the videos as a class at a later time.

- Each group takes a turn conducting the test:
  - Materials Managers place the pumpkin inside the package, seal it, and drop it.
  - Timekeepers open the package after it lands.
  - Speakers describe how the pumpkin looks after being dropped.
  - Recorders complete the Test Results page.
- Encourage the class to ask questions and have the Speaker answer their questions, either during that group's turn or after the group's video is presented. Sample questions:

  Before the test or video:

  Which materials did you use?

  What was one change your group made to the original plan?

  What was one challenge your group faced?

  After the test or video:

  Overall, was your design successful? How do you know?

  What part of your design would you improve?

  Would your package design work for a larger or heavier pumpkin?
- Have each student complete a Checklist sheet.

Opportunities for Differentiation

To make it simpler: Provide each group with a cardboard box large enough to hold the pumpkin. Allow students to add materials to the inside of the box to protect the pumpkin.

To make it harder: Add a criterion that the pumpkin must remain undamaged after three drops (instead of just one). Add another test, such as kicking the package, or use hollowed-out pumpkins (jack-o-lanterns).

Names _____

_____

_____

_____

Pumpkin Package Test Results

1 Did your pumpkin go in
and out without damage ?   Yes   No

2 Was it easy to put the
pumpkin in and take it
out?   Yes   No

3 Did your pumpkin stay in
its package when
dropped?   Yes   No

4 Was the pumpkin safe
after it was dropped?   Yes   No

5 Does the package have
four materials?   Yes   No

Name _____

Pumpkin Package Checklist

❶ Did I do my job in the group?

Yes   Sort of   No

....

❷ Did I help to build the pumpkin package?

Yes   Sort of   No

....

❸ Did I show that I understand properties of pumpkins?

Yes   Sort of   No

....

❹ Did I use the properties of materials in the design?

Yes   Sort of   No

Engineering
Native American Style Drums

Criteria for Product

- Must make a sound when tapped with hands
- Must hold together after 20 taps

Constraints for Challenge

- Drums must be played with hands, not drumsticks
- May use only materials provided in the kit, but may get more of those materials by bartering with other groups
- Must complete each design process stage within the time limits

Challenge

Native Americans have used drums throughout history in entertainment and rituals, and to send warnings. Students design and build drums.

Materials

Drum Materials (for each group)

- 3 balloons of different sizes
- 1 sheet of felt
- 1 rolled oats container or coffee can (same item for each group)
- 2 ft. of plastic wrap
- 2 paper lunch bags
- 3 paper plates
- 5 sheets of plain paper
- 1 large sheet of tissue paper
- 1 plastic shopping bag (to use as a material)
- 1 roll of clear tape
- 2 ft. of waxed paper
- 1 yd. of yarn
- 10 rubber bands
- 1 shopping bag (to hold kit)

Tools

- Box cutter (teacher use only)
- Can opener (teacher use only)
- Hole punch
- Scissors
- Tape measures

Additional Materials

- Examples of drums
- Computer and projector
- Document camera (optional)
- Job cards (page 10)
- Chart paper
- Markers
- Pencils
- Paper

Before You Begin

- Learn about sound as part of the regular science curriculum.
- Locate images of drums online using the search phrase "Native American Drums." Also include videos showing examples of drums in use, if desired.
- Cut off the bottoms of the oats or coffee containers.
- Prepare a materials kit for each group by placing all drum materials in a shopping bag.
- Make two copies of the Brainstorm (page 43) and one copy of the Checklist (page 45) for each student.
- Make a copy of the Test Results (page 44) for each group.
- Make a set of job cards (page 10) for each group.
- Set up the timer where students can check it.
- Display the Criteria for Product and Constraints for Challenge where students can see them.

Get Set

5-Step Process

1 ▸ Investigate
45 minutes

- Hand around the examples of drums for students to examine and try.
- Explain to students that Native Americans have been making and playing drums for thousands of years. Show students the images and videos of drums that you found. As a class, discuss what these drums have in common and how they are different.
- Explain to students that the Pilgrim settlers at the Plymouth colony learned a lot from the Native Americans. Tell students that they will design their own drums using what they've learned by observing Native American drums and by studying sound. Ask students:

  What shape are most drums? Why do you think this is?

  What parts does a drum have?

  How does a drum make a sound?

  Do some materials work better than others in creating sound?

  What questions do you have about the challenge?

- Review with students the Criteria for Product and Constraints for Challenge, as well as the time limits for Brainstorm, Plan, and Build.

2 ▸ Brainstorm
30 minutes

- Display the Drum Brainstorm sheet so that all students can see it. Point out that a drum has three parts: a base, a top, and something that connects the top and the bottom.
- Pass around the contents of one materials kit. Allow students to investigate the materials. Explain that their group will receive these materials in these quantities to build their drum.

- Give each student two copies of the Brainstorm sheet. Tell them to create four different designs for a drum and write the materials chosen for each part on the label lines.

- Tell students that they need to think about the best design for a base, a top, and a connection. Instruct students to work alone quietly for 10 minutes.

- While students brainstorm, walk around the room. Offer starting places for students who are stuck and ask guiding questions to support detailed work. Suggested questions:

  What materials have properties that are good for that part of the drum?

  Can the drum base be cut down? If so, should it be? Why?

  What material(s) might work for the top of the drum?

  How will you connect the top of the drum to the bottom?

  Does the top need to be loose or tight to make a sound?

  Did you leave the bottom open or closed? Why?

- Explain that bartering was part of many Native American cultures. Bartering means to make a trade. For this challenge, if a group needs more of a material than is in the kit, they may offer something in trade.

3 ▶ Plan
45 minutes

- Consider the learning modalities among your students—for example, whether each is a kinesthetic, visual, or auditory learner or shows another strong learning preference. Create groups of three to four students so that there are different learning styles in each group. Do not consider academic level when forming groups for this challenge.

- Once children are grouped, tell them that it is time to choose jobs. Each job suits people with different strengths. For example, students who like to talk usually make great Speakers. Students who are organized make terrific Timekeepers. People who like to work with their hands make excellent Materials Managers. And people who focus on details, keep good notes, and are good artists make fantastic Recorders.

- Explain that each group has students with different strengths. Hand out the job card sets. Instruct students to discuss their strengths within the group and decide who should take each job. (For groups with three students, one student takes two jobs.)

- After students have chosen their jobs, set the timer for 20 minutes and tell groups to begin planning their drums. Encourage students to talk about one part of the drum at a time, to listen to each person's favorite idea, and to come up with one choice as a group for building each part of the drum.

- Remind Timekeepers that it is their job to make sure the group stays on task and completes each stage of the design process on time.

- Empower the Speaker by reminding students that if a disagreement occurs, the Speaker may make the final decision. The Speaker is the only group member allowed to get the teacher involved.

- As students discuss, circulate around the room to offer support as needed and to help settle disagreements. Ask questions to encourage thinking. Sample questions:

  How similar or different were your original designs?

  How did you decide which materials to use?

  What properties of the materials did you consider when you decided? Why are those properties important for the drum to make a sound?

  Does everyone agree? Was it difficult to get everyone to agree?

- After a group has chosen a design, each member draws one version of the group's final plan on a separate sheet of paper. After comparing to be sure all plans look alike, the Recorder draws and labels a large diagram on a piece of chart paper. This is the version everyone in the group follows while building.

4 ▶ Build
60 minutes

- Tell students they will now work as a group to build and test their drums. Remind them that everyone helps to build the drum, in addition to doing their jobs. Set the timer for 60 minutes. Remind Timekeepers to keep track of the time and let the group know if they need to speed up to finish.

- Each Materials Manager picks up the materials kit for the group. If a group needs to barter for materials with another group, the Materials Managers handle it.

- Remind students to follow their group's plan exactly. Students should work little by little, testing the drum as they work. If something does not work as planned, students may change their drum. It is the Speaker's job to tell the teacher about the change and explain why it is being made. The Recorder adjusts the plan using a different color.

- As students work, walk around the room, helping to drive progress. Praise students for collaborating well together. Ask guiding questions to support critical thinking skills. Sample questions:

  How is each person participating?

  Does everyone feel they are contributing equally?

  Is the drum coming out the way you thought it would?

  Did you need to measure anything? If not, should you?

  Have you bartered with another group? What did you trade?

  Has your group made any changes to your plan?

  Have you tested your drum yet? What did you learn?

- Place finished drums in a safe place for storage until it is time to present.

5 ▶ Test & Present

15 minutes prep, then 5 minutes per group

- Tell the class that this time, they will think of the questions to ask of each group. Encourage students to share ideas as a class. List questions where everyone can see. Sample questions might include:

    What materials did you choose for each section?

    What challenges did you face?

    How many times did you change your plan?

    If you had more time, what would you improve?

- Guide students to review questions and, as a class, choose the best five. Leave only those five questions on the list. Remind students that each group must answer all five questions.

- Call the first group and give the Recorder a Test Results sheet.

- Turn on the document camera or other projection device. Have the Materials Manager place the drum under the camera so all students can see it projected. Alternatively, have the Manager carry the drum around so all students have a chance to see it up close.

- When all students have seen a group's drum, the group tests the drum and the Recorder completes the Test Results sheet.

- When all groups have presented, give each student a Checklist sheet to complete.

Opportunities for Differentiation

To make it simpler: Demonstrate a method for attaching the top of the drum to the bottom— for example, lay a top on the base and wrap it with rubber bands. Tell students that they need to choose the material for the top and a way to attach it to the drum.

To make it harder: Add more items to the materials kits and instruct groups to create a set of two or more drums. Or add a constraint that the drum must be loud enough to hear from 10 feet away.

Name _____

Native American Style Drum Brainstorm

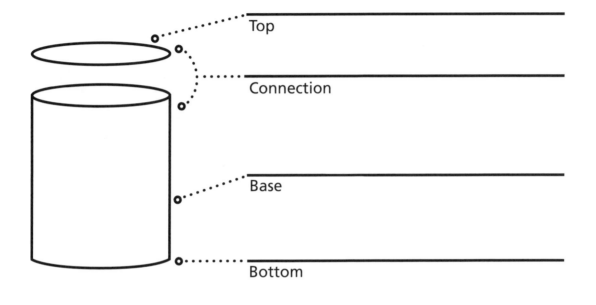

Top _____

Connection _____

Base _____

Bottom _____

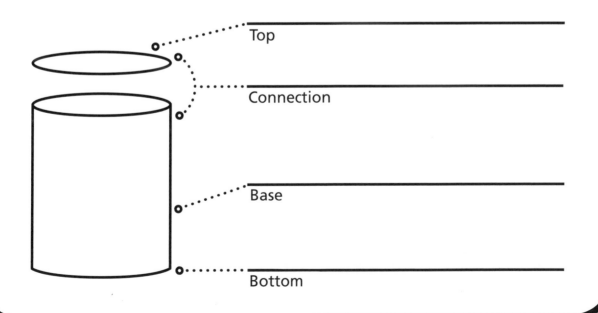

Top _____

Connection _____

Base _____

Bottom _____

Names _____

_____

_____

_____

Native American Style Drum Test Results

❶ Did your drum make a sound when tapped with hands?

Yes   No

....

❷ Did your drum hold together after 20 taps?

Yes   No

....

❸ Where is the best place to play your drum?

Floor   Lap   Between legs

....

❹ Why is that the best place?

_____

Name _____

Native American Style Drum Checklist

❶ I used what I know about sound to design the drum.

    Yes   Sort of   No

....

❷ I helped design the drum with my group.

    Yes   Sort of   No

....

❸ I helped to build the drum.

    Yes   Sort of   No

....

❹ I did all the parts of my group job.

    Yes   Sort of   No

Engineering

Thanksgiving Snack Assembly Lines

Challenge

Industrial engineers design assembly lines to break large jobs into smaller pieces so the whole process gets finished more quickly. Students design and use assembly lines to speed up the preparation of Thanksgiving Snacks.

Criteria for Product

- The table must be set with four complete place settings
- A place setting includes a plate, a bowl on top of the plate, a cup to the right of the plate, and a folded napkin to the left of the plate
- Every serving of the snack mix must contain every ingredient
- An equal amount of snack mix must be served in each bowl
- Each cup must contain cranberry juice
- The snack must be assembled and served in 15 minutes

Constraints for Challenge

- All group members must clean hands before packages are opened
- Students must not open packages or set up any materials before beginning
- Only materials provided in the materials kit, plus one bonus item, may be used
- Must complete each stage of the design process within time limit

Materials

Snack Ingredients (for each group)

- 1 bag popped popcorn
- 2 kinds of Chex cereal
- 1 bag of chocolate chips
- 1 bag of sweetened dried cranberries
- 1 bag of nuts
- 1 bottle of cranberry juice

Note: *Omit nuts if nut allergies are a concern in your classroom. Disposable dishes recommended.*

Table Settings and Tools (for each group)

- 4 bowls
- 4 cups
- 4 napkins
- 4 plates
- Hand wipes
- Measuring cup
- Mixing spoon
- Scissors

Bonus Items (for each group)

- 1 large bowl
- Set of 5 small bowls
- 1 lunch or serving tray

Additional Materials

- Computer with Internet access
- Computer projector
- Chart paper
- Job card sets
- Shopping bags for materials kits (paper or plastic)
- Digital timer
- Digital video camera (optional)

Before You Begin

- Encourage families to contribute ingredients and dishes for the snack. The challenge works best if each group has whole, unopened bags and bottles. Another approach is to repackage ingredients in quantities that are slightly greater than those in the recipe, so students still have to measure.

- Locate and bookmark Internet videos of assembly lines for the Investigate stage. Examples include the "How we make chocolate" videos at the Hershey's Company site (www.hersheys.com) and the Jelly Belly Virtual Factory Tour (www.jellybelly.com). For a nonfood related product, search YouTube for historical footage of the Ford Model T assembly line.

- Prepare a materials kit for each group. Include all materials from the Snack Ingredients and Table Settings and Tools lists. Place all items in one or more shopping bags.

- Clear off tables and decide how best to arrange them. Each group needs a prep area to work in, a table on which to set and serve the snack, and clear passage between the two.

- Make a copy of the Snack Recipe (page 50) and Test Results (page 51) for each group.

- Make a copy of the Checklist (page 52) for each student.

- Make a set of job cards (page 10) for each group.

- Write the numbers 1, 2, 3, and 4 on slips of paper so that each group has a set of numbers 1 to 4.

5-Step Process

① Investigate
45 minutes

- Remind students that Native Americans and the Pilgrims worked together to prepare and serve the famous Thanksgiving feast that we remember and celebrate each year.

- Ask students to share memories of times when a job was made easier because of teamwork. For example, have they worked with family members to wash dishes or fold laundry?

- Describe the idea of an assembly line. Show a video of a factory or professional kitchen where a food product or other product goes through different phases in its creation.

- Tell students that they have the challenge of designing an assembly line to make a Thanksgiving snack, set the table, and serve the snack.

- Show students a materials kit. Tell them that, in addition to the items in the materials kit, each group may choose one item from the Bonus Items list. Point out that a set of five small bowls counts as one item.

- Review with students the Criteria for Product and Constraints for Challenge, as well as the time limits for Brainstorm, Plan, and Build.

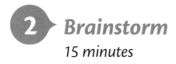

Brainstorm
15 minutes

- The whole class will brainstorm together for this challenge. Ask the class to list smaller jobs that make up the large task—for example, making the snack mix, measuring it into the bowls, setting the table. Each of the smaller tasks can likewise be broken down further. Make a list of the smaller tasks where students can see it. Ask students:

    What smaller tasks make up the big task of preparing and serving the snack?

    Do any tasks need to happen in a certain order?

    What tasks can be done at the same time?

    Do you think it's faster to have one person complete an entire task, or to divide big tasks into smaller parts?

    Where will you prepare the food items? How will you move them?

Plan
30 minutes

- Organize groups of three to four students who work well together. Try to place friends together in groups for this challenge.
- Provide each group with a copy of the Snack Recipe, a set of job cards, and a set of number slips 1 to 4.
- Students in each group take turns choosing a number. The person who chooses 1 gets to pick a job first. Job choice continues in order until the person with number 4 takes the remaining job. Students may not trade jobs, but groups of three may decide who gets the extra job. Remind students of their job responsibilities (page 7).
- Tell students that they will not write down their plans for this challenge. Instead, group members will describe their tasks before the group presents their assembly line.
- Let students begin planning as soon as they've chosen jobs. Set the timer for 20 minutes when the last group is ready. As students talk, stop by and check with each group. Ask guiding questions. Sample questions:

    Which tasks will each of you take on?

    How will you make and serve the snack? Will you mix all the ingredients together, or put some of each ingredient in each bowl?

    What will you choose as your Bonus item? Why will you choose that?

    How can you avoid spills even though you will be working quickly?

- The plan will not be written down this time; instead, students will describe their tasks during the Test & Present portion of the challenge.

Build
25 minutes

- Tell students that all groups will start at the same time to build their assembly lines for the snack. First they will get their materials.
- Assign each group a table to set and a separate place to put their materials. Check that each group has about the same distance from their prep area to their table.
- Have Materials Managers pick up a materials kit and the Bonus item that their group agreed on. Give each Recorder a Test Results page.

- Groups may unpack their kits and place items in their prep area, but they cannot get started until you say "go."
- Instruct Timekeepers to call out the remaining time throughout the snack prep, and to say "done" when their group is finished.
- When all groups are ready, set the timer for 15 minutes and say "go." As students work, stay out of the way and observe. Students need to focus on the assembly line process.
- As each group finishes, ask the Recorder to note on the Test Results page how much time is left on the timer.

5 ▶ Test & Present

5–10 minutes per group

- Write these questions where the class can see them. Give each group time to discuss their answers.

  What was your process for preparing the snack?

  Who did each task in the process?

  How did you set the table?

  How long did it take your group to complete each task?

  What would you do to improve your time if you did it again?

- As soon as each group is ready, give them a video camera.
  - The Recorder makes the short video (no longer than 3 minutes).
  - The Materials Manager holds up the materials during the video.
  - The Speaker does most of the speaking.
  - The Timekeeper states how long it took to prepare the snack and set the table.
- Alternatively, groups may present to the class without recording.
- When a group has finished presenting, they may eat their snacks and then clean up.
- Hand out a Checklist sheet to each student after cleanup is finished.

Opportunities for Differentiation

To make it simpler: Omit the table setting from the challenge. Guide groups step-by-step through the Plan stage. Provide pre-measured ingredients and omit measuring cup.

To make it harder: Add a constraint that states that students must first set the table, then create the snack, then serve the snack. This will make it harder to finish in time.

Thanksgiving Snack Recipe

(Makes 4 servings)

2 cups popped popcorn
1/2 cup nuts
1/2 cup chocolate chips
1 cup Chex cereal (1/2 cup each of 2 kinds)
1/2 cup dried sweetened cranberries

Place Setting

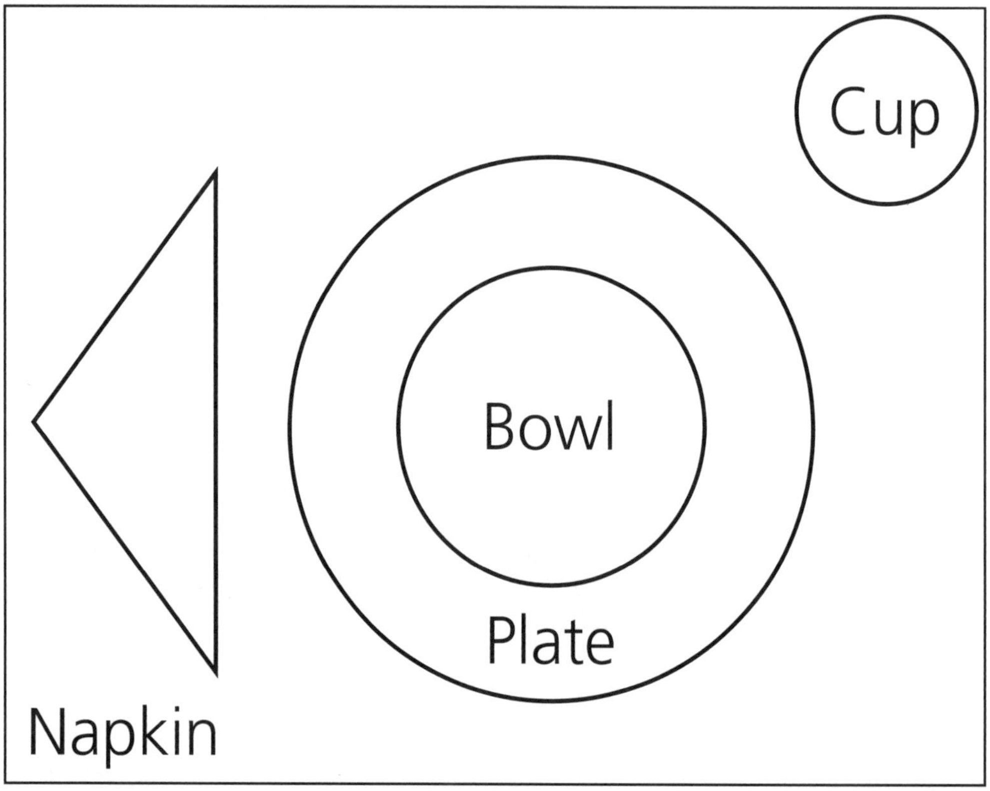

Cup

Bowl

Plate

Napkin

Names _____

_____

_____

_____

Thanksgiving Snack Assembly Line Test Results

❶ Did everyone clean their hands first?　　　　Yes　　　No

....

❷ Is the table set correctly?　　　　Yes　　　No

....

❸ Do all bowls have each ingredient?　　　　Yes　　　No

....

❹ Do all bowls have the same amount?　　　　Yes　　　No

....

❺ Do all cups have juice?　　　　Yes　　　No

....

❻ How much time was left?　　　　____minutes
　　　　____seconds

Name _____

Thanksgiving Snack Assembly Line Checklist

❶ I listened to the ideas of others.

Always   Sometimes   Not at all

....

❷ I shared my ideas with the group.

Always   Sometimes   Not at all

....

❸ I showed I understand how an assembly line works.

Yes   Sort of   No

....

❹ I did my job and I worked on the assembly line.

Yes   Sort of   No

Engineering
Candy Houses

Criteria for Product

- Must be built on the base provided
- Must have four walls and a roof
- Must have a door, but it does not have to open
- Must be at least 6 inches tall
- The entire house must be made of edible materials
- Must have three or more different objects for landscaping (for example, fence, mailbox, tree)
- Exactly seven items from the building materials list must be used

Constraints for Challenge

- Must complete each stage of the design process in time allowed

Challenge

The gingerbread man needs a place to live! Candy houses have been part of fairy tales and tradition for hundreds of years. Students work as civil engineers to design and build gingerbread-style candy houses.

Materials

Base Materials
(for each group)

- 1 house base (tray or foil-covered cardboard)
- 1½ cups stiff icing (recipe page 57)

Building Materials

- To be determined during class Brainstorm
- Alternatively, work from the Ideas list (page 57)

Tools
(for each group)

- 6 craft sticks
- Ruler
- Scissors
- 1-qt. freezer bag
- A few plastic spoons
- A few paper or plastic bowls

Additional Materials

- Computer and projector
- Chart paper
- Markers
- Mixing spoons
- Mixing bowls
- Food coloring
- Job cards (page 10)
- Digital timer

Before You Begin

- Purchase or make stiff icing (recipe page 57).
- Prepare a building base for each group.
- Decide whether you want to brainstorm a class materials list before getting materials, or if you prefer to gather materials from the Ideas list (page 57) in advance. Either way, prepare to contact families and ask for donations, or plan to go shopping.
- Locate online and download several pictures of candy houses. Helpful search terms include "candy house" and "gingerbread house." Think outside the box and search for "gingerbread beach house," "gingerbread castle," or similar variations.
- Make a copy of the Test Results (page 58) for each group.
- Make a copy of the Checklist (page 59) for each student.
- Make a set of job cards (page 10) for each group.
- Display the Criteria for Product and Constraints for Challenge.

Get Set

5-Step Process

1 ▶ Investigate
50 minutes

- Read a story that involves a candy house, such as *The Gingerbread Baby* by Jan Brett.
- Tell the students that the gingerbread man has run away again! To bring him home, we need to build a house for him.
- Display the pictures of different gingerbread and candy houses, pointing out the different foods that are used for different parts of the house and yard. Ask students:

    What parts does a candy house need?

    What can you use to hold a candy house together?

    Do all candy houses need to be the same?

    Do you have any questions about this challenge?

- Review with students the Criteria for Product and Constraints for Challenge, and the time limits for Brainstorm, Plan, and Build.

2 ▶ Brainstorm
15 minutes

- As a class, talk about different foods that could be used to build a candy house. Make a list of student suggestions where all students can see it. Ask:

    What could you use for the walls and roof of the house?

    What makes good pavement for a walkway? What makes a good fence?

- Alternatively, you may provide materials similar to the ones on the Ideas list (page 57), either by shopping or by asking students to each bring in some items. Then display the building materials and brainstorm as a class which materials could be used to build each part of a candy house.

3 Plan

40 minutes

- Make groups of three to four by placing students of different learning modalities together (kinesthetic, visual, auditory, or others). Give each group a set of job cards (page 10; Speaker, Materials Manager, Timekeeper, Recorder).

- Explain that each group will decide who does which job. Guide students to think about the things each group member is good at. Support students as they decide which jobs each member should do.

- Remind students of the responsibilities of each job (page 7). Confirm that the Timekeeper is responsible for all time management and task assignments.

- Tell students that, for this challenge, the Materials Manager makes final decisions about which materials to use if the group can't decide.

- Also for this challenge, the Recorder jots down ideas as the group plans. Once a decision is made, the Recorder draws the plan on chart paper using a different color for each building material. The rest of the group helps with labels and with writing a key to the color codes.

- Set the timer for 30 minutes. While students are working, walk around the room and talk with each group. Ask guiding questions. Samples:

    What are you using for the walls of your house? Why did you choose that?

    How can you get the walls to stick together?

    What items will be in your yard? What shape is that object? What food has that same shape?

    When you build, what part will each of you work on?

    Are you stuck on anything? What can I help with?

4 Build

60 minutes

- Tell students they will now work as a group to create their candy houses. Set the timer for 60 minutes.

- Assign each group a place to build and provide a base to build on.

- Have Materials Managers collect the items in their group's plans from the table.

- Make sure students remember that if there are any changes to the plan, the Speaker needs to notify the teacher and get permission before continuing, and the Recorder needs to note the changes on the plan.

- As students work, continue to offer support. Suggested questions:

    Is every person doing a fair share of the work?

    Are all the materials working out the way you imagined?

    What are you doing right now? How is that helping the group?

    Are you working on one piece at a time or are you building parts separately and bringing them together at the end?

    What can you do to make sure you finish on time?

- When complete, place candy houses in a safe place to dry and harden.

Test & Present

10 minutes discussion, then 5 minutes per group

- Ask students to list some questions that would be good to ask of each group. Write all questions where students can see them.
- Guide students to review the questions and, as a class, choose the best five. Leave only those questions on the list. Sample questions:

  How did you come up with the idea for this design?

  What properties does that food have that made you choose it?

  What is your favorite part of your house?

  Did you have any surprises while you were building?

- Tell students that each group must answer all those questions during their presentations, as well as demonstrate that their house meets the criteria.
- Turn on a document camera (if available) and give a Test Results sheet and a ruler to the first group. Have them place their candy house under the camera so that it is projected onto the screen, large enough for all students to see. Have students follow the Test Results sheet to present their houses. If the document camera offers a recording option, use it to record the presentations.
- Provide each student with a Checklist after presentations are finished.

Opportunities for Differentiation

To make it simpler: Provide students with the Ideas list. Allow students to use as many or as few items as they choose. Give students something to support the center of the house, such as a half-gallon milk carton that has been cut down. Students can attach walls to the center, rather than making walls stand on their own.

To make it harder: Give students a budget to work within. Add measurements for length and width to the criteria. Require a certain number of windows or exact items for the yard. Challenge students to design a nontraditional candy house, such as a beach house, igloo, apartment building, or school.

Ideas for Candy House Building Materials
For reference during Brainstorm, or to use as a shopping list

House Walls
- Graham crackers
- Fudge stick cookies
- Marshmallows
- Mini candy bars
- Pretzel logs
- Sugar cubes

Walkway Paving
- Lifesavers
- Necco wafers
- Ritz crackers
- Vanilla wafers

Garden Wall & Fence
- Jolly Ranchers candy
- Marshmallows
- Mini candy bars
- Pez candy
- Twisted pretzels
- Pretzel sticks

Trees & Shrubs
- Ice cream cones
- Lollipops
- Spearmint leaf gumdrops

House Decorations
- Candy canes
- Gumdrops
- Gummi candies
- Sno-Caps candy
- Jellybeans
- M&M'S
- Skittles
- Smarties
- Red Hots
- Mini marshmallows

Stiff Icing Recipe
(Enough for 3–4 houses)

6 cups confectioners' sugar (about 2 pounds)

½ teaspoon cream of tartar

4 egg whites

In one bowl, sift together confectioners' sugar and cream of tartar. Use an electric mixer to beat egg whites lightly in a separate large bowl. Add confectioner's sugar to egg whites a little at a time while beating. Continue to beat for about 5 minutes or until mixture is thick enough to hold its shape.

Place about 1–1½ cups of icing in a freezer-grade resealable plastic bag for each group. When it is time to build the houses, cut a tiny bit off one corner of the bag so that students can squeeze the icing out.

Names _____

_____

_____

_____

Candy House Test Results

❶ Circle all the things the house has.

Base   4 walls   Roof   Door

❷ How tall is the house?   ___ inches

❸ Is the house edible?   Yes   No

❹ What objects are in the yard?

_____   _____

_____   _____

❺ We used these 7 foods:

_____   _____

_____   _____

_____   _____

_____

Name _____

Candy House Checklist

❶ I listened when others talked.

    Always   Sometimes   Not at all

....

❷ I shared my ideas with the group.

    Always   Sometimes   Not at all

....

❸ I helped build the house.

    Yes   Sort of   No

....

❹ I helped solve any problems that came up.

    Yes   Sort of   No

....

❺ I did all my jobs.

    Yes   Sort of   No

....

❻ Something I did that I'm proud of is

_____.

Engineering
Candle Holders

Criteria for Product

- Must hold a candle upright
- Candle must sit tight—no sliding or tipping
- Must sit on a table
- Must be pretty to look at

Constraints for Challenge

- Designs cannot be related to any specific holiday
- Can choose materials only from those provided
- Must stay within budget of 25¢ for manufacturing costs
- For safety reasons, the candle may not be lit
- Each stage of the design process must be completed within the allowed time

Challenge

Lights and candles are a central part of cultural celebrations all over the world. Students design and build functional and decorative candle holders.

Materials

Candle Holder Materials (for class)

- Aluminum foil
- Modeling clay (sticks or 1½-in. balls)
- Ceramic tiles
- Decorative wrapping paper
- Tissue paper in assorted colors
- Pipe cleaners
- Glass jars
- Metal cans
- Paper bags
- Small stencils

Candle Options (for each group)

- Pillar
- Taper
- Tea light
- Votive

Tools

- Clear acrylic spray (teacher use only)
- Decorative hole punches (optional)
- Paint
- Paintbrushes
- Permanent markers
- Scissors with decorative edges (optional)
- White glue

Additional Materials

- Computer with Internet access
- Computer projector
- Various candle holder examples
- Pennies (25 per group)
- Job card sets (page 10)
- Chart paper
- Markers
- Plain paper
- Pencils

Note: *Items on Candle Holder Materials list are suggestions. Substitutions are allowed, and quantities may be whatever is readily available.*

Before You Begin

- Study winter holidays as part of your regular curriculum.
- Recruit an adult volunteer to serve as shopkeeper, if desired.
- Locate and bookmark a couple of candle-related websites, such as YankeeCandle.com or candles4less.com.
- Divide modeling clay into sticks or roll into balls about 1½ inches in diameter.
- Set all candle holder materials and tools out on a table.
- Make signs for the price of each material. See price list on page 62.
- Choose a container to collect pennies students "spend" on materials.
- For each group, set up one envelope with 25 pennies.
- Make a set of job cards (page 10) for each group.
- Make a copy of the Test Results (page 65) for each group.
- Make a copy of the Checklist (page 66) for each student.
- Display the Criteria for Product and Constraints for Challenge where students can see them.

5-Step Process

 **Investigate**
30–40 minutes

- Ask students to recall craft projects they've done that involved decorating things.
- Ask students to think of places and times that they have seen candles and candle holders. Display a candle-related website that you bookmarked in Before You Begin. Look under accessories for votive holders, and show students some examples. Ask students:

    What do you observe about the candle holders on this site?

    Why do people need or want candle holders?

    What questions do you have about the challenge?

- Provide candle holders for students to examine. Include examples of candle holders for pillars, votives, tea lights, and tapers. Explain to students that they will design and build a candle holder for one of these candle types.
- Allow students to examine the different styles of candles that will be available.
- Talk to students about their experiences with buying things. Tell students that each material for this challenge has a price. Each group will be given 25¢ to buy materials. That means the group's planned candle holder can cost no more than their budget of 25¢. Tools and planning materials are provided for free.
- Review with students the Criteria for Product and Constraints for Challenge, and go over the time limits for Brainstorm, Plan, and Build.

Candle Holder Material Prices

Bags	2¢ each
Cans	5¢ each
Jars	6¢ each
Clay	3¢ each
Tiles	6¢ each
Pipe cleaners	1¢ each
Stencils	3¢ each
Foil	2¢ for 1 foot
Tissue paper	2¢ for 1 foot
Wrapping paper	2¢ for 1 foot

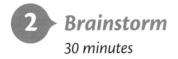

2 ▸ Brainstorm
30 minutes

- Invite students to come to the table in small groups to look at the materials and their prices. Ask students:

  Which candle will you choose for your candle holder?

  What are some properties that these materials have?

  How could these materials hold up a candle?

  Can you change the shape of any materials?

  Would that material burn if the candle were lit? Is there a way you can use it so that it won't be near the flame? (Candles will not be lit in school, but students should consider this while designing.)

- Give each student a blank sheet of paper. Have students fold the paper in half from top to bottom and then again from left to right so it has four sections when opened. Have students write "Brainstorm" at the top.

- Instruct students to work quietly by themselves for 15 minutes. Their task is to choose one candle style, think of four designs for a candle holder for that one candle, and draw one design in each section of the paper. Encourage them to add labels that show the materials used.

- While students brainstorm, walk around the room. Offer starting places for students who are stuck and ask guiding questions to support detailed work. Suggested questions:

    Which candle style will you work with? Why did you choose it?

    Which material will you use for that part? Is it the best choice? Why?

    How will you decorate your candle?

    Is this candle holder better for decoration or to use for light?

    How much will this candle holder cost to make?

③ Plan
40 minutes

- Invite students to stand in large groups based on which type of candle they chose (taper, pillar, votive, or tea light). Then move from group to group, looking for similarities in designs. Create smaller groups of three to four students based on these similarities.
- Explain that each group has students with similar designs for the same kind of candle. Hand out job card sets and instruct students to take 5 minutes to decide which student should take each job. While deciding, they should think about what each group member is good at doing.
- Once students have chosen jobs, set the timer for 20 minutes and let them begin planning.
- Tell students to place their Brainstorm pages on the table where everyone in the group can see them. Ask them to look for ways that the designs are similar. From there, they should start their group plan.
- Encourage groups to use additional pieces of paper to jot down ideas as they talk.
- Walk around the room, checking in on conversations to make sure that students are being respectful, staying on task, doing their chosen jobs, and working well together. Sample questions:

    How similar or different were your designs?

    How did you decide which materials to use? Why did you decide on those?

    Is everyone in agreement? Was it difficult to get everyone to agree?

    Have you considered all the criteria for product?

- After each group agrees to a plan, instruct them to write up a shopping list and add up the cost of materials. If they are over budget, then they need to change their design.
- Once the group has a final plan, each group member draws his own version of it on a separate sheet of paper. After comparing to be sure all plans look alike, the Recorder draws a large version on chart paper.

4 ▶ Build

30 minutes

- Tell students it is time to build their candle holders. Set the timer for 30 minutes. Each Materials Manager brings the group's shopping list and receives a money envelope to purchase materials from the table, where an adult serves as shopkeeper.

- Remind groups to follow their plans. If a plan changes, the Materials Manager must figure out if the budget will cover the change. Then the Speaker must get permission from the teacher, and the Recorder must draw the change on the plan. This process is time-consuming, so the Timekeeper needs to let the group know right away if there is not enough time to even ask for a change. This process will help reinforce that it is better to make changes during the Plan stage.

- As students work, walk around the room, checking the progress of each group. Praise students for working together well. Sample questions:

    How is each person participating?

    Why did each person get each job?

    Is the design coming out the way you planned it?

    Have you made any changes to your plan?

    How long did it take to make your change?

- Place finished candle holders in a safe place until any paint or glue is dry.

5 ▶ Test & Present

5 minutes per group

- Tell students that each group will get to ask one question of every group presenting.

- Ask the first group to come up to the front of the room with their candle holder. Give the Recorder a Test Results sheet.

- Ask the Materials Manager to demonstrate how the holder meets the criteria.

- Invite students to ask questions. Allow five questions per group.

- When all groups have finished, provide each student with a Checklist.

Opportunities for Differentiation

To make it simpler: Provide only a votive or tea light, which is small and stable even without a holder. Show students two or three specific ways to build and decorate a candle holder and allow them to pick from those ideas. Limit the choice of materials so students are not overwhelmed.

To make it harder: Provide only a taper and add a criterion that the candle must rise above the top of the holder. Or ask students to design a holder for three of the same type of candle that still meets all other criteria.

Names

_____

_____

_____

Candle Holder Test Results

❶ Is the candle upright?   Yes   No

....

❷ Does the candle sit tight in
   the holder?   Yes   No

....

❸ Does the holder sit on the
   table?   Yes   No

....

❹ Is the candle holder pretty?   Yes   No

....

❺ How much did it cost to make?   _____

....

❻ How much under budget is it? (How much
   money was left over?)

                25¢ - _____ ¢ = _____ ¢

Name _____

Candle Holder Checklist

❶ I shared my ideas with the group.

Always   Sometimes   Not at all

❷ I listened to the ideas of others.

Always   Sometimes   Not at all

❸ I showed I understand the Criteria and Constraints.

Yes   No   Not sure

❹ I did all parts of my job.

Yes   No   Not sure

Engineering
New Year's Noisemakers

Challenge

As we ring in the New Year, celebrations include excitement and noise! Students design and build new kinds of noisemakers.

Criteria for Product

- Must be made from recyclable materials
- Must fit into the test box (about 10 x 8 x 6 inches)
- Must have two or more ways to make noise
- Noise can be heard from a distance of 5 feet

Constraints for Challenge

- May use only the materials provided
- Must use only one item from each set of materials
- Must meet deadlines for each stage of the process

Noisemaker Materials (for class)

Set 1
- Cans
- Paper towel and bath tissue rolls
- Cereal boxes
- Small foil pie pans
- Plastic tubs
- Plastic bottles
- Paper bags
- Paper cups
- Paper plates

Set 2
- Balloons
- Pipe cleaners
- Rubber bands
- Yarn

Set 3
- Craft sticks
- Plastic spoons

Set 4
- Newspaper
- Cellophane or Mylar
- Waxed paper
- Rice
- Beans

Tools
- 3 rolls of masking tape
- 2–4 bottles of white glue
- 1 set of permanent markers
- Paint
- Paintbrushes
- Hole punch
- Scissors
- Rulers
- Staplers

Additional Materials
- Sample noisemakers
- Construction paper
- Chart paper
- Markers
- Job cards (page 10)
- Pencils
- Plain paper
- Tape measure
- Box for test, about 10 x 8 x 6 in.

Note: *Gather materials in quantities that are readily available.*

Before You Begin

- Complete any unit on sound that is part of the regular curriculum.
- Contact families to arrange for donations of clean recyclables.
- Obtain a variety of inexpensive noisemakers from a party store or other source. Avoid those that are put into the mouth.
- Display materials on a table, grouped in sets as shown in the list. Make labels for items for student reference, if desired.
- Display the tools in a separate area.
- Make a copy of the Test Results (page 72) for each group.
- Make a copy of the Checklist (page 73) for each student.
- Make a set of job cards (page 10) for each group.
- Display the Criteria for Product and Constraints for Challenge so the class can see them.

5-Step Process

Investigate
15–20 minutes

- As a class, talk about New Year celebrations and noisemakers. Noisemakers are common at some sports games, as well as at New Year's. Ask students to share stories about noisemakers they've heard and used.
- Display some commercial noisemakers. Allow students to examine and try them.
- Tell students that they have been invited to take on an important job. Because there is no money to purchase noisemakers for an upcoming celebration, the students will have to design them. Ask students:

  How do these noisemakers we've been using make sounds? Do they all make sound the same way, or are they different?

  Can one noisemaker make more than one sound?

  Is the noisemaker louder if you use more force, or less force?

  What do you know about making noise from other experiences?

  What questions do you have about the challenge?

- Review with students the Criteria for Product and Constraints for Challenge, and the time limits for Brainstorm, Plan, and Build.

Brainstorm
30 minutes

- Show students the materials on the table and invite students to come in small groups to look. Point out the different sets, and explain that those will be important during planning. Ask students:

  What are some properties that these materials have?

  How could you use each of these materials in a noisemaker?

  Can you change the shape of some of these materials?

  Can you use one material in more than one way?

Do any of the materials make noise on their own?

Can any materials make noise if they're combined with another material?

- Give each student two sheets of plain paper. Have them fold both sheets in half lengthwise and widthwise to make four boxes, then label one sheet Materials List and the other one Brainstorm. Have them label the boxes on the Materials List Set 1, Set 2, Set 3, and Set 4.
- Instruct students to look at each set of materials. They need to choose one item from each set that they would like to use to build a noisemaker, and then either write its name or draw it on their Materials List.
- Have students work for 10 minutes to design noisemakers that include all four of their chosen items. They should draw four different designs on their Brainstorm sheet, each in a different section, with each design using the same four materials from their list.
- While students brainstorm, walk around the room and check in on each student. Ask guiding questions to help students who are stuck, and to encourage students who are rushing through to slow down and think about details. Suggested questions:

  What gave you the idea to do it that way?

  Which material will you use for that? Is it the best choice? Why?

  How will your noisemaker make one sound? How will it make another sound?

- Have each student circle one favorite design.

3 ▶ Plan
40 minutes

- Ask the class to think about their favorite noisemaker design. How will the noisemaker work? Will they shake it, blow on it, bang it, or crumple it? Ask the class to divide into four groups: shakers, blowers, bangers, and crumplers. Assist any students who aren't sure where they belong; for example, if they stomp, place them with crumplers. If they use two methods, help them to choose one.
- Invite students to further divide themselves into smaller groups of three to four.
- Pass out job cards to each group. Tell students to choose jobs, but do not tell them how. Make sure students understand the responsibilities of each job (page 7).
- Tell students to place their brainstorming pages on the table so that everyone can see all designs. Ask them to look at the designs for similarities and start there with a group plan. Set the timer for 20 minutes of Plan time.

- Circulate around the room. Listen to conversations. Continue to walk around the room, checking in with groups. As needed, ask guiding questions to help students plan. Sample questions:

  Did you choose one person's idea or did you take pieces of all designs?

  What experience do you have with these materials that helped you choose?

  How did you share ideas? How did you make sure everyone had a voice?

- After each group agrees to a plan, each student in the group draws her own version of the final plan on a sheet of paper. Students should compare the versions to be sure they match. If they do not, they need to discuss until they agree on one plan.

Build
30 minutes

- Tell students they will now build their noisemakers. Call the Materials Managers up to collect the materials. Set the timer for 30 minutes.

- Remind students that they planned their designs as a guide to follow, but that plans can and do change sometimes. If they need to change their plans, the Speaker must first get permission from the teacher. Then the Recorder needs to update the design. The Timekeeper needs to keep everyone on task even while a change is happening.

- As students work, circulate and visit with each group. Praise students for excellent problem-solving efforts. Ask guiding questions to support critical thinking skills. Sample questions:

  Are you testing as you go or waiting until the end?

  Do you know if your noisemaker will fit in the box?

  Is that working the way you expected it to?

  Can you think of two ways to make your noisemaker work?

- Place finished noisemakers in a safe place until it is time to test and present.

Test & Present
10 minutes per group

- Set up an area to test the noisemakers. Distance is part of the test, so it may be helpful to work in a hallway, in a gymnasium, or outdoors. Mark off every 5 feet for a distance of 15 to 25 feet.

- Ask the first group to come up to the front of the room with their noisemaker. Give the Recorder a Test Results sheet. Invite students in other groups to ask questions. Allow five questions per group.

- Set up a test of the noisemaker. Have the Materials Manager stand at one end of the testing area.

  - The Materials Manager places the noisemaker in the test box to see if it fits.

  - The Timekeeper walks 5 feet away and faces away.

- The Materials Manager uses the noisemaker one way. The Timekeeper says whether he can hear the noise, and the Recorder writes down the answer.
- The Materials Manager uses the noisemaker the other way, and results are recorded.
- If the first test worked, the Timekeeper walks another 5 feet and the test is repeated.
- When all groups have tested their noisemakers, return to the classroom and give each student a Checklist.

Opportunities for Differentiation

To make it simpler: Show some examples of noisemakers built using the materials, and provide a small number of options to change each sample design. For example, show students how they can create a shaker by placing small objects inside a larger object, but let them choose which large object and smaller objects to combine.

To make it harder: Do not pre-sort the items into sets, but still allow students to take only four materials. Or increase the distance from which the noisemaker can be heard. Or require the noisemakers to make sound three different ways, rather than two.

Names _____

_____

_____

_____

New Year's Noisemaker Test Results

1 Does your noisemaker fit in the box?

_____

2 What are the 2 different ways it makes noise?

_____   _____

3 Can someone hear the first noise from 5 feet away?

_____

4 Can someone hear the second noise from 5 feet away?

_____

5 How far away can the noisemaker be heard?

_____ feet

Name _____

New Year's Noisemaker Checklist

❶ I offered my ideas to the group.

    Always   Sometimes   Not at all

....

❷ I listened to the suggestions of others.

    Always   Sometimes   Not at all

....

❸ I used what I know about sound in my design.

    Yes   No   Not sure

....

❹ I did my job and I helped to build the noisemaker.

    Yes   No   Not sure

Engineering
Snowman
Huts

Criteria for Product

- Must have four walls and a roof
- Must cover the snowman top to bottom
- Must be removable and replaceable
- Must fit in the bowl provided
- Must keep the snowman from melting

Constraints for Challenge

- May not be attached to the bowl
- May use only materials provided in the kit, but may trade with other groups
- Must meet time limits for each stage of the process

Challenge

Every winter people build snowmen, but as soon as the weather warms, the snowmen melt. Students design and build huts to place around model snowmen to keep them from melting.

Materials

Snowman Hut Materials (for each group)

- 1 ft. of aluminum foil
- 1 ft. of plastic wrap
- 1 sheet of construction paper
- 2 paper towels (thick)
- 1 ft. of waxed paper
- 1 ball or stick of modeling clay
- 1 sheet of felt
- 1 sandwich bag full of hay or straw
- 10 craft sticks
- 1 yd. of masking tape
- 2 foam cups
- 1 foam or paper bowl (must be flexible)
- 1 shopping bag (paper or plastic)

Tools

- Rulers
- Scissors
- Plastic medicine measuring cups (1 oz. or 5 ml)

Additional Materials

- Books about snow and snowmen (optional)
- Ice cubes
- Ice chest (teacher use)
- Large plastic cups (to hold snowmen)
- Heat lamp (optional)
- Chart paper
- Markers
- Paper
- Pencils
- Job cards (page 10)
- Digital timer

Before You Begin

- Make enough trays of ice cubes for each group to have three cubes, plus a few extras.
- Make model snowmen. For each snowman, moisten three ice cubes with warm water, stick them together in a stack, and place upright on a tray lined with waxed paper or foil. Make enough snowmen for each group plus a few extras. Place tray in a freezer until ready to use. Transfer snowmen to an ice chest to bring to the classroom.
- Divide modeling clay into sticks or roll into balls about 1½ inches in diameter.
- Prepare a materials kit for each group, following the materials list. Place materials in a shopping bag. Wind masking tape around a craft stick before placing it in the bag.
- Make a set of job cards (page 10) for each group.
- Make a copy of Observations (page 79) and Test Results (page 80) for each group.
- Make a copy of the Checklist (page 81) for each student.
- Display the Criteria for Product and Constraints for Challenge where students can see them.

5-Step Process

 **Investigate**
45 minutes

- Invite students to share experiences with building snowmen and watching them melt. If your students have no experience with snow, read books about playing with snow, such as *The Snowy Day* by Ezra Jack Keats; *Snow* by P.D. Eastman; *Snowmen at Night* by Carolyn Bueher; or any book of Frosty the Snowman.
- Tell students that their next engineering challenge is to design a hut to keep a snowman from melting. Of course, real snowmen can be very large, and snow isn't always available. So they will work with small models. Explain that scientists and engineers also build small models to test how well their ideas work.
- Show one of the ice-cube snowmen, and explain that each group will have one to work with. Then show them the materials available in one kit. The challenge is to build a hut that will keep the snowman from melting. Ask students:

  What are some ways we keep things cold?

  How do you keep food cold when you go on a picnic?

  Can a material that keeps something warm also keep something cold?

  What kinds of things help keep you warm?

  What questions do you have about the challenge?

- Review with students the Criteria for Product and Constraints for Challenge, and the time limits for Brainstorm, Plan, and Build.

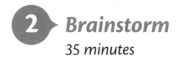

2 ▶ Brainstorm
35 minutes

- Divide students into groups of three to four based on similar learning modalities (kinesthetic, auditory, visual, or others).
- Tell students that this time, they will Brainstorm as a group. But each group member will still draw her own ideas. Display a materials kit for students to look at. Tell them each group will have only the materials in one kit, but groups may trade with other groups.
- Circulate through the room, asking questions to prompt thinking. Suggested questions:

  What are some properties that these materials have?

  How could you use these materials to make a snowman hut?

  How could you change the shape of some of these materials to make them work for you?

  Could you layer these materials on top of each other?

  How could you use a flexible material to make a wall, if the wall has to be stiff?

- Once students are familiar with the materials, allow 20 minutes for thinking up as many designs as they can for a hut that keeps a snowman from melting. Explain that they should work on their own designs, but they may talk with group members as they work. Encourage students to label diagrams with the materials they plan to use.
- While groups brainstorm, listen in on their conversations. Ask questions to deepen the discussion and offer a different point of view. Suggested questions:

  Is it easier or harder to brainstorm with a group (instead of by yourself)?

  What are some ways to build the walls?

  How tall will your hut be? How wide?

  How can you check that your hut design is tall enough for a snowman?

3 ▶ Plan
30 minutes

- Review the responsibilities of each job (page 7): Speaker, Timekeeper, Materials Manager, and Recorder. Pass out job cards to each group and invite students to choose jobs.
- Tell students it's time to come up with one plan that they all agree to build. Set the timer for 30 minutes. The Recorder draws ideas in pencil on a large sheet of chart paper that the group can see.
- If a plan needs more of one material, then the Speaker should find the Speakers in other groups to discuss the needed material and what they have to trade. No trade should be made yet, just an agreement to make the trade.
- Circulate throughout the room, looking at plans. Ask questions to better understand student thinking and to push students to think about previous experiences that apply. Sample questions:

What experiences do you have with snowmen that can help you with your design?

What experiences do you have with these materials?

How do you know the hut will fit on the snowman?

Is everyone sharing and working during planning?

How can you get more of a material if you need it for your design? Which group member should set that up?

- Once the plan is finished, students should use markers to color code and label the materials used in the group's plan.

4 ▶ Build
30 minutes

- Tell students it is time to build the huts. Set the timer for 30 minutes and have Materials Managers collect kits for their groups. Materials Managers also make any trades that the Speakers arranged.

- When a group needs to check the size of their hut, the Materials Manager may use a plastic cup to borrow a snowman from the ice cooler (it will be too cold to carry by hand). Snowmen should be returned to the cooler as quickly as possible.

- Remind students that their plan is the basis for building. If the plan changes as they build, the Speaker notifies the teacher and the Recorder updates the plan using a different color.

- Continue to monitor work. Praise students and encourage teamwork. Ask guiding questions to develop ideas further, such as:

    Is there something that you are good at that you are doing to help build the snowman hut? What are the others in your group doing?

    Why did you decide to use those materials?

- Place finished huts in a safe place until the presentation time. Return the snowmen to the freezer.

5 ▶ Test & Present
50 minutes

- Tell students that all groups will test their huts at the same time. Set up the heat lamp if you plan to use one.

- Explain to students that each group will have 5 minutes to present their designs during the snowman test. Between groups, everyone will check their snowmen. Explain that when they check, it is important not to spill any water that melted from the snowmen.

- Give each group a snowman model in a foam or paper bowl, an Observations page, and a Test Results page. The Recorder should describe what the snowman looks like at 0 minutes.

- The Timekeeper places the hut around the snowman and places the hut in the test area.

- Once all huts are in place, set the timer for 5 minutes and call on the first group. Ask the group to show their hut (without taking it off the snowman), explain why they chose the materials they did, and why they think their hut design will work. Invite students from other groups to ask questions. Allow three questions per group.

- When the timer goes off, all groups lift the huts and check on their snowmen. All group members discuss what they see. The Recorders write a few words on the Observations page to describe what the snowman looks like, such as "no melting," "some melting," or "lots of melting."

- Have students replace the huts. Set the timer for another 5 minutes.

- Allow another group to share.

- Continue this procedure until all groups have shared and the snowmen have been checked and measured at least four times.

- At the end of the presentations, tell students that each group will measure the water that melted from their snowman. Remove the hut from one snowman and show how to carefully bend the bowl to make a pouring spout. Pour the water into a medicine measuring cup. Have students observe and record the amount of water using the units on the cup, which may be teaspoons, ounces, or milliliters. Have the Recorder write down the measurement.

- Have the Recorder complete the Test Results page with the group's help.

- Give each student a Checklist to complete.

- Schedule a later time to discuss the recorded results and to determine which snowman melted least. While reviewing the results, ask students:

    Which snowman melted the least?

    How do you know?

    Why do you think that snowman melted the least?

    Did the size of the hut have anything to do with success?

    Which materials worked best to keep the snowman from melting?

Opportunities for Differentiation

To make it simpler: Provide students with a prebuilt craft-stick frame for the hut. Students then decide which materials to use to fill in the walls.

To make it harder: Include a requirement that the snowman must be visible through the hut.

Names _____

_____

_____

_____

Snowman Hut Observations

Time	Observations
After 0 minutes	
After 5 minutes	
After 10 minutes	
After 15 minutes	
After 20 minutes	
After 25 minutes	
After 30 minutes	

Names _____

_____

_____

Snowman Hut Test Results

❶ Does it have 4 walls? _____

....

❷ Does it have a roof? _____

....

❸ Does it cover the snowman top to bottom? _____

....

❹ Is it removable and replaceable? _____

....

❺ Does it fit in the bowl? _____

....

❻ How much of the snowman was melted into water after 30 minutes? ___ oz./tsp./ml (circle the unit you used)

Name _____

Snowman Hut Checklist

❶ I was a strong member of the group.

Yes   Sort of   Not at all

....

❷ I used good time management.

Always   Sometimes   Not at all

....

❸ I used what I know about heat, cold, and materials.

Yes   Not sure   No

....

❹ I showed I understood the Criteria and Constraints.

Yes   Not sure   No

Engineering
Groundhog Shadow Hiders

Criteria for Product

- Must hide a shadow under any kind of light
- Groundhog must face "out" of the shadow hider
- Must stand by itself
- Must be easy to set up and use
- Must be something built by the group (not found)

Constraints for Challenge

- All materials must be available in the classroom
- Must meet deadlines for each stage of the process
- Must be able to use tools with no help from the teacher
- Must not cause problems for any living things

Challenge

The Groundhog Day legend says that when the groundhog sees his shadow, it means another six weeks of winter. Students design and build devices to prevent the groundhog from seeing his shadow, no matter how sunny it is.

Materials

Shadow Hider Materials

- Any items available in the classroom

Tools

- Any tools available in the classroom

Additional Materials

- Job cards (page 10)
- Chart paper
- Markers
- Paper bag
- Plain paper
- Pencils
- Flashlights
- Digital timer
- Groundhog (stuffed toy)
- Digital video camera (optional)

Before You Begin

- Complete any unit on shadows that is in your curriculum.
- Collect several flashlights to have available during the challenge.
- Acquire or borrow a stuffed toy groundhog.
- Figure out how many groups your class needs in order to have three to four students in each. Write each group number on slips of paper, so there is one slip for each student. For example, 23 students make five groups of 4 and one of 3. Make four slips with number 1, four more with number 2, and so forth, but only three slips with number 6.
- Scout the school grounds for a shadow hider test site. You need an open area that is both sunny and available at the time of day you plan to test.
- Make a set of job cards (page 10) for each group.
- Make a copy of the Presentation Questions (page 87) and Test Results (page 88) for each group.
- Make a copy of the Checklist (page 89) for each student.
- Display the Criteria for Product and Constraints for Challenge where students can see them.

5-Step Process

 **1** **Investigate**
45 minutes

- Provide flashlights and allow students to explore and investigate shadows. Suggested questions to prompt investigation if needed:

  What makes a shadow?

  Which objects or materials cast shadows? Which do not?

  Are shadows from sunlight different from shadows from flashlights?

  Which way does a shadow point?

- Remind students of the Groundhog Day legend. Talk to students about the idea that it's fun to pretend we can make spring come six weeks early. Invite students to think of ways to make that happen. If students do not suggest the idea that they could hide the groundhog's shadow, guide the discussion to that conclusion.

- Tell them that this is their challenge: design and build a device to hide the groundhog's shadow. Ask students:

  What are some materials you would need to hide a shadow?

  How could you test your shadow hiders without a groundhog?

  What questions do you have about the challenge?

- Show students the toy groundhog so they are familiar with its size. Review with students the Criteria for Product and Constraints for Challenge, as well as the time limits for Brainstorm, Plan, and Build.

2 ▶ Brainstorm
35 minutes

- Tell students they will get into small groups to brainstorm materials for this challenge. To form groups, students draw numbers out of a bag. Students with the same numbers are in the same group.

- Provide each group with a large piece of chart paper and four markers. Tell them that they will have 20 minutes to brainstorm. Ask students:

  What is needed to make a shadow?

  How can you hide a shadow?

  What materials do you need to create a shadow hider?

  How can you use each of these materials?

- Tell students to think of anything and everything that is in the classroom that might help with building a shadow hider. If a student asks whether any materials are off-limits, say that you will let them know later. For Brainstorm, it's okay to think of using anything.

- Ask students to talk in their groups and offer suggestions. When the group agrees with an idea, then the person with the idea can write or draw it on the chart paper.

- Remind students they are not planning yet. They are simply thinking of anything that might help. Encourage them to be "messy" with ideas, words, and drawings all over the paper. This is not the time to rule out things. It's better to think about how a suggested item might be used.

- Walk from group to group, looking at each chart paper and asking about the group's thinking. Ask guiding questions that push students beyond their initial ideas and stretch their imaginations. Suggested questions:

  Will you use light? Where will the light come from?

  What will you use that material for? What will it do?

  Have you thought about items in a cabinet that you could take out?

- After 20 minutes, pass out job cards to each group and tell students to choose jobs. Remind students about the responsibilities of each job (page 7).

3 ▶ Plan
30 minutes

- Tell the students it's time to review the brainstorming page and discuss all the ideas to create a group plan. As a group, they should come to a decision about how their shadow hider will meet the criteria. Set the timer for 30 minutes.

- Walk around the room, facilitating the work. Ask guiding questions to help students plan and to use their knowledge of shadows to design the device. Sample questions:

  What makes a shadow appear? How will this design stop that from happening?

  Does everyone agree on this design?

  Who thought of this part? What was your thinking when designing this part?

- As you walk, also make sure that you approve of the materials each group is planning to use. Ask students to find a substitute for any material that is "off-limits."
- When a group has reached a decision, each student draws a diagram of the final plan on a separate sheet of paper. All plans within a group must look the same. If they do not, then let the group know that they've had some miscommunication. They need to review their plans until everyone understands and agrees.

4 ▶ Build
40 minutes

- Tell students it's time to build the shadow hiders. Point out that flashlights are available for testing their shadow hiders as they build. Set the timer for 40 minutes.
- Materials Managers collect all the necessary items. Only materials listed in the group's plan can be used.
- Remind students that the plan their group made is like their blueprint. All good builders follow the blueprint. Tell them that following the blueprint doesn't always work the first time, so they might need to adjust it. If they make an adjustment, the Speaker tells the teacher and the Recorder changes the plan so it shows the actual finished product. Recorders should make changes in a different color or draw a new plan, labeled Plan 2.
- Instruct the Timekeeper to watch the timer and update the group on how much time is left. Let the group know that the Timekeeper is in charge of keeping the task moving and making sure everything is finished on time, so it's important to cooperate.
- Walk around and stop by each group to see how things are progressing. Encourage students to let everyone in the group take part in the build. Sample questions:

    What do you know about shadows? How did you use that information in your design?

    Did you need to measure anything, or check the size of it?

    Will everything hold together well enough?

    What is the hardest part of building this device?

    Have you tested your shadow hider?

- Place finished shadow hiders in a safe place until it's time to present.

 **5** **Test & Present**

15 minutes per group

- On a sunny day, lead the class outdoors to the test site. Bring the shadow hiders and the groundhog toy.
- Give each Speaker a copy of the Presentation Questions. Give each Recorder a copy of the Test Results.
- Set up a test area. Place the toy groundhog on the ground, standing up, and check to see that its shadow is visible.
- Inform the groups that each Timekeeper will make a video of their group's presentation. Hand the first group's Timekeeper the video camera.
- Have the Speaker read the "Before the Test" questions from the Presentation Questions sheet, or you may read them to the Speaker. Have the Speaker answer each question aloud.
- Instruct the Materials Manager to set up the group's shadow hider.
- Tell the Speaker to read and answer the "During the Test" questions.
- Observe the results of the shadow hider test, and prompt the Recorder to write them down.
- Prompt the Speaker to answer the "After the Test" questions.
- Invite students to ask any questions they have. Limit additional questions to three.
- Repeat until all groups have tested and presented.
- Distribute Checklist sheets to all students.
- If allowed by your district's policies, and if you have permission from parents, publish the video to an approved, secure website. Show students how to find and play the video.

Opportunities for Differentiation

To make it simpler: Work with students as a class to devise a basic design for the shadow hider. From there, charge student groups with the task of coming up with different materials to use, and with altering the shadow hider to improve it.

To make it harder: Limit the number of classroom materials students are allowed to use. Add more test sites, or test at two different times of day, so that students can be sure the shadow hider works anywhere.

Groundhog Shadow Hiders
Presentation Questions

Read each question. Then say the answer for your group.

Before the Test

❶ How well did our group work together?

❷ How does our shadow hider work?

❸ Did we follow our plan or did we make changes?

❹ What changes did we make?

During the Test

❺ Is it working the way we planned?

❻ Can we see the groundhog's shadow?

❼ Are there changes we would make if we could?

After the Test

❽ Are we happy with our design?

❾ How could we improve our design?

Names _____

_____

_____

_____

Shadow Hider Test Results

❶ Is the groundhog facing out of the shadow hider? _____

❷ Does the shadow hider hide the groundhog's shadow? _____

❸ Does the shadow hider stand by itself? _____

❹ How easy was the shadow hider to set up and use?

Very easy   Kind of easy   Not easy

❺ On a scale of 1 to 5, rate this shadow hider.

1	2	3	4	5
Not good	Okay	Good	Very good	Excellent

Give two reasons you picked that number:

_____

_____

Name _____

Shadow Hider Checklist

Rate how well you did.

❶ I helped design it and I let others help, too.

1	2	3
Yes	Sort of	Not really

❷ I helped the group finish on time.

1	2	3
Yes	Sort of	Not really

❸ I used what I know about shadows in the design.

1	2	3
Yes	Sort of	Not really

❹ My understanding of how to hide shadows is

1	2	3
Very good	Good	Not good

Engineering
Valentine Mailboxes

Criteria for Product

- Must be made from recyclable materials
- Must stand by itself, not be attached to a wall
- Must have a door that opens and closes easily
- Must hold five standard-sized cards and a small candy box
- Must stand with cards and candy box inside

Challenge

With Valentine's Day coming, the mail carrier will have heavier loads than usual. Mailboxes will be stuffed full! Students design and build mailboxes that are easy to use and durable.

Constraints for Challenge

- Must use exactly 10 items (for example: 1 cereal box, 2 cardboard tubes, 1 bag, 3 rubber bands, 2 craft sticks, and 1 sheet of paper)
- Must meet deadlines for each stage of the engineering design process

Materials

Mailbox Materials (for class)

- Assorted large cans
- Assorted cardboard boxes
- Assorted plastic bottles
- Assorted plastic tubs
- Construction paper
- Pipe cleaners
- Newspapers
- Paper bags
- Paper cups
- Paper plates
- Cardboard tubes from paper towels and bath tissue
- Rubber bands
- Wood craft sticks
- Yarn
- Clear tape
- Masking tape

Tools

- Permanent markers
- Hole punch
- Scissors
- Rulers

Additional Materials

- Computer and projector
- 1 small candy box
- 5 greeting cards
- Digital timer
- Job cards (page 10)
- Chart paper
- Markers
- Plain paper
- Pencils
- Document camera (optional)

Note: *Gather materials in whatever quantities are readily available. Substitutions are allowed.*

Before You Begin

- Contact families to ask for donations of clean recyclables.
- Acquire five standard-sized greeting cards and a small candy box for testing the mailboxes. A box of candy hearts or a four-piece box of chocolates is a good size. Decide whether to empty the box before allowing students to test their mailboxes with it.
- Search online for images of mailboxes. Commercial sites that sell mailboxes are good sources, as the focus is on the shape and size of the mailbox, not its decoration.
- Set out all mailbox materials and tools on a table.
- Make a copy of the job cards (page 10) for each group.
- Make a copy of the Test Results (page 95) for each group.
- Make a copy of the Checklist (page 96) for each student.
- Display the Criteria for Product and Constraints for Challenge where students can see them.

5-Step Process

1 ▶ **Investigate**
45 minutes

- Use a computer and projector to display photos of mailboxes in a variety of shapes and sizes. Discuss with students the characteristics that these mailboxes have in common. Ask students to share their ideas about what a mailbox should look like and what it needs to be able to do.
- Remind students that Valentine's Day is coming! That means lots of cards and candy going through the mail. Tell students that they have a new challenge. The mail carrier needs some new mailbox designs to hold all those Valentine cards and treats. Ask students:

    What is a mailbox's job? What does it need to do?

    How can you make it easier for the mail carrier to deliver letters and packages?

    Where on a mailbox can you place a door? Are all mailbox doors in the same place?

- Review with students the Criteria for Product and Constraints for Challenge, as well as the time limits for Brainstorm, Plan, and Build. Point out that, although some of the mailboxes in the pictures are mounted on walls, the mailboxes they design need to stand up by themselves.

2 ▶ **Brainstorm**
20 minutes

- Show students the table of available materials. Ask students:

    What are some properties that these materials have?

    How could you use these materials to make a mailbox?

    How could you change the shape of some of these materials to make them work for you?

- Remind students that they must use exactly 10 items in their mailbox design—no more and no fewer.
- Provide students with sheets of blank paper. Ask them to write "Brainstorm" across the top. Tell students to fold their papers to make four sections. Instruct students to work alone quietly for 10 minutes to design four different mailboxes, drawing one in each section.
- Remind students to count the items they use in each design to be sure they have exactly 10. Ask them to label each item.
- Move throughout the room, commenting on designs. Ask guiding questions to encourage students who are rushing to focus on details and to help students who are having difficulty coming up with ideas. Suggested questions:

  Where will the door for your mailbox be?

  Which material will you use for that part of the mailbox?

  How will this design make it easier for the mail carrier to make deliveries?

  How do you know the cards and candy box will fit in your mailbox?

③ Plan
40 minutes

- Tell the class that they will be allowed to form their own groups this time. Remind them that a group should have a mix of people who are good at doing different things.
- Invite students to group themselves in threes and fours. Assist students who are having difficulty finding a group, or who are trying to form a group that is too large.
- Review the responsibilities of each job (page 7). Pass out job cards to each group. Explain to students that, for this challenge, it is up to the group to decide how to choose or assign jobs. Walk around the room. Listen to student conversations about jobs, but do not interject. Allow students to work out issues on their own.
- After all the students in a group have chosen their jobs, tell them it is time to come up with one group plan. Set the timer for 30 minutes. Have students place their Brainstorm pages on the table where everyone in the group can see all designs.
- Check in with each group and ask guiding questions to help students plan and extend thinking. Sample questions:

  How did you decide on the plan? Where did all the ideas come from?

  Have you checked to be sure you have exactly 10 items?

  Have you started thinking about who will do each part, when you build the mailbox?

- After a group agrees to a design, each student in the group draws his own version of the final plan on a separate sheet of paper. All plans in a group must look alike. If they do not, students need to discuss and revise the plan.

4 ▶ **Build**
40 minutes

- Tell students they will now collaborate (work together) to create their mailboxes. Set the timer for 40 minutes. Invite Materials Managers to gather materials from the table.
- Remind students to follow the group plan for as long as it works for them. If the plan no longer works, the Speaker should let the teacher know how the plan will change. When the teacher approves, then the Recorder should update the plan to show the actual finished product.
- Remind Timekeepers to watch the time remaining and to make sure that their group manages time well.
- Continue checking in with each group. Encourage students to share responsibilities and work as a group. Ask guiding questions to support critical thinking skills. Sample questions:

  What is each person's responsibility as you build?

  Why are you putting the mailbox together that way?

  Are you testing as you go, or are you waiting until the end?

- Place finished mailboxes in a safe place until it is time to test and present.

5 ▶ **Test & Present**
10 minutes per group

- Post the Presentation Directions (page 94) where all groups can see them, or copy them onto a sheet of paper for each group to borrow.
- Tell students that they will ask the questions for these challenge presentations.
- Ask the first group to come up to the front of the room with their mailbox. Give the Recorder a Test Results page.
- Allow the Speaker to direct the rest of the team, using the Presentation Directions. (Assist in reading the directions as needed.) The Materials Manager sets up the mailbox and makes it stand, the Timekeeper tests the mailbox, and the Recorder writes down the results.
- Invite students to ask questions. Allow five questions per group.
- When all groups have finished, distribute a Checklist sheet to every student.

Opportunities for Differentiation

To make it simpler: Provide students with a basic design for the mailbox that does not have a stand or a door. Allow students to modify the basic design so it meets the Criteria for Product. The constraint limiting the number of materials can also be removed.

To make it harder: Add a requirement to the Criteria for Product that the mailbox must stand at a certain height from the floor.

Mailbox Presentation Directions

❶ Set it up.

❷ Make it stand.

❸ Open the door.

❹ Put in the mail.

❺ Close the door.

Names _____   _____

_____   _____

Valentine Mailbox Test Results

❶ Does the mailbox stand by itself?

Yes   No

....

❷ Is the door easy to open and close?

Yes   No

....

❸ Did all the items fit inside the mailbox?

Yes   Kind of   No

....

❹ Was it still standing with the items inside?

Yes   No

....

❺ How would you rate this mailbox?

1	2	3
Not good	Good	Very good

Give three reasons for your answer:

_____

_____

_____

Name _____

Valentine Mailbox Checklist

Rate how well you did.

❶ I helped design it and I let others help, too.

1	2	3
Yes	Sort of	Not really

⋯⋯⋯⋯⋯⋯⋯⋯⋯⋯⋯⋯⋯⋯⋯⋯⋯⋯⋯⋯⋯⋯⋯⋯⋯⋯⋯

❷ I helped the group finish on time.

1	2	3
Yes	Sort of	Not really

⋯⋯⋯⋯⋯⋯⋯⋯⋯⋯⋯⋯⋯⋯⋯⋯⋯⋯⋯⋯⋯⋯⋯⋯⋯⋯⋯

❸ I kept working when things went wrong.

1	2	3
Yes	Sort of	Not really

⋯⋯⋯⋯⋯⋯⋯⋯⋯⋯⋯⋯⋯⋯⋯⋯⋯⋯⋯⋯⋯⋯⋯⋯⋯⋯⋯

❹ I used materials well and did not waste them.

1	2	3
Yes	Sort of	Not really

⋯⋯⋯⋯⋯⋯⋯⋯⋯⋯⋯⋯⋯⋯⋯⋯⋯⋯⋯⋯⋯⋯⋯⋯⋯⋯⋯

❺ I helped my group clean up.

1	2	3
Yes	Sort of	Not really

Engineering
Kites

Criteria for Product

- Must lift off the ground at least 5 feet when pulled or placed in the wind

Constraints for Challenge

- May use only the materials provided
- Must stay within budget of 25¢
- Must stay within time limits for each stage of the process

Challenge

March means windy spring weather! Students design and build kites to enjoy in the March winds.

Materials

Kite Materials (for class)

- 25 sheets of tissue paper
- 1 roll of waxed paper
- 1 roll of aluminum foil
- 10 plastic trash bags
- 25–50 lunch-size paper bags
- Plain paper
- Construction paper
- 50–100 craft sticks
- 50–100 straws
- 1 dozen ¼-in. wood dowels
- 50 ten-in. barbecue skewers
- A few rolls of masking tape
- A few rolls of clear tape
- 1 roll of string

Note: *Quantities are approximate and may be adjusted.*

Tools

- Rulers
- Tape measures
- Scissors
- Hole punches

Additional Materials

- Chart paper
- Markers
- Pencils
- Plain paper
- Digital timer
- Job cards (page 10)
- Pennies (25 per group)
- Envelopes or small bags (for pennies)
- Kite string (1 roll per group), for flying kite
- Board or plastic pipe, 5 ft. or longer (optional)
- Computer with Internet access
- Computer projector

Before You Begin

- Study wind and how it moves things as part of your regular curriculum.
- Recruit one or more adult helpers for the day that kites are tested.
- Locate examples of kite-flying videos. Suggested sites for online videos: 5min.com; activitytv.com (search for "diamond kite," "sled kite," "barn door kite"); pbskids.org/teachers (search for "trash bag kites"); pbskids.org/dragonflytv (search for "kites").
- Select a safe outdoor location for testing the kites. It should provide room for students to run and should be free of overhead obstructions, such as trees and power lines.
- Mark a board, plastic pipe, or other portable item (5 feet or longer) in 1-foot increments, for use during testing. Colored tape or wide-tipped marker works well. You may use relative measurements instead; see Test & Present.
- Figure out how many groups of three to four students are in your class. For example, 23 students make five groups of 4 and one of 3. Make four slips of paper with number 1, four with number 2, and so forth, but only three slips with number 6. Place all slips in a bag.
- For safety reasons, trim sharp points off skewers using scissors or nail clippers.
- Place kite materials on a table. Make signs for the price of each material, if desired.
- Make a copy of the Observations (page 103) and Test Results (page 104) for each group.
- Make a copy of the Price List (page 102) and Checklist (page 105) for each student.
- For each group, place 25 pennies into an envelope or bag.
- Display the Criteria for Product and Constraints for Challenge.

5-Step Process

1 *Investigate*
40 minutes

- As a class, discuss students' experiences with kites and what it takes to make kites fly. Let students know that their next challenge is designing kites.
- Ask students to name some other devices that rely on wind power (for example, paper airplanes, wind vanes, wind socks, planes, gliders, windmills). Encourage them to think about how they can use their prior knowledge to design a kite that really flies.
- View one or more videos about kite building and flying. Ask students:

  What shapes might make good kites? Why do you think so?

  What properties does a kite need so it can fly?

  What holds a kite together?

  What are some questions you have about the challenge?

- Allow students to touch and examine the kite materials so they can base their decisions on the materials' properties.
- Review with students the Criteria for Product and Constraints for Challenge, as well as the time limits for Brainstorm, Plan, and Build.

2 ▶ Brainstorm
20 minutes

- Give each student a copy of the Kite Materials Price List and a sheet of plain paper. Explain that they do not have to pay for the string to fly the kites.
- Tell students they have 15 minutes to brainstorm different designs for a kite, using the materials available. They will work by themselves.
- Remind students that designing can be "messy" work and you don't expect their designs to be perfect. It is important for them to think of as many ideas as possible, rather than to focus on one perfect drawing.
- Encourage students to think about kite shape and materials as they design. It is more important to think about the kite's shape than to focus on its decorations.
- Walk around the room, looking at each paper and asking about each student's designs. Ask guiding questions that push students to access prior knowledge and to think about measurement and dimensions. Suggested questions:

    How long will that part be? How wide?

    Why did you choose that material?

    Is this design like anything you've seen or built before?

    Can you think of another shape for a kite?

- After 15 minutes, ask students to circle their favorite or best design.

3 ▶ Plan
40 minutes

- Take out the bag of group numbers that you set up before the challenge. Explain that students will draw numbers out of the bag. The number they get is the group they'll be in. Let each student choose a number from the bag. Place all students with the same number in the same group.
- Ask students to choose jobs within their groups. Review the responsibilities associated with each job (page 7).
- Set the timer for 30 minutes. Instruct students to take turns sharing their kite designs. They need to discuss how to combine their ideas into one design that the whole group will build. Point out the Materials Price List and remind students they must stay within budget.
- Check in with each group, complimenting good collaboration and asking guiding questions to help students stay on task and improve their designs. Sample questions:

    How did you decide on this part of the design?

    Will you need to change something else about the kite because of this change?

    Why did you choose to use this material instead of another?

    Does this kite design need a tail? Why do you think so?

    What do you know about wind that has helped you with this plan?

    Do you know how big this kite will be?

    Have you planned to buy enough of this material? How can you be sure?

    Are your materials within budget?

- As groups finish, hand out plain paper to each student. Explain that each group member should draw a picture of the group's plan. All plans within a group need to match.

4 ▶ Build
45 minutes

- Decide whether you will allow groups to go over budget if any materials need replacing as they build. Let students know in advance.
- Tell students it's time to build the kites. Set the timer for 45 minutes.
- Give 25 cents to each Materials Manager. Invite them to come shopping for the materials their group has planned to use.
- Remind students that they should refer to the plan for the entire Build. If something in the plan will not work, they may change the plan. But the Speaker must first get the change approved by the teacher, and the Recorder needs to show the change in the plan, so that the plan shows the finished product.
- Keep up with the progression of each group. Get involved in discussions, but do not offer suggestions. Encourage students to let everyone help build the kite. Ask guiding questions that remind students to use their science knowledge. Sample questions:

    How does air move things?

    Is there any way to control the wind?

    Where will you attach the string to fly the kite?

    What are you doing to make sure your kite doesn't fall apart?

    Have you had any unexpected challenges yet? What did you do to solve them?

- Place finished kites in a safe place until the presentation time.

5 ▶ Test & Present
40 minutes total for Test; 3–5 minutes per group for Present

- With your adult helper, take the students outdoors. Bring kites, kite string, Observations sheets, pencils, and the 5-foot measuring stick, if you're using one. Lead students to the test site. Explain briefly why this is a good site for kite flying. Ask students to list some obstacles (trees, power lines, buildings) that would not be good for a kite-flying site.
- Direct each group to find an open area to test their kites in. Take turns if space is limited.
- Hold up the measuring stick in a central location. (Instead of a measuring stick, you may use relative measurements such as "up to the teacher's knees," or "higher than the teacher's head." If you choose this approach, you will need to adjust how Recorders write down the test results accordingly.)
- Tell students that each group member takes a turn with the kite:
    - One student flies the kite.
    - Another student holds the kite up to help get it started.
    - A third student observes how high the kite flew.

- The fourth student marks how high the kite flew on the Observations bar graph.

- Back indoors, have groups complete the Test Results page, then take turns presenting their results. Invite students in other groups to ask questions. Limit the number of questions per group as needed.

- Have each student complete the Checklist.

Opportunities for Differentiation

To make it simpler: Use the Internet and other resources to locate some basic kite designs; allow students to choose one as a starting place. Ask them to make changes or adjustments to that design to improve its flight. Remove the budget constraint.

To make it harder: Include specific size Criteria or Constraints for the kite, such as length, width, or length of tail. Or put cards showing various shapes (such as triangles, rectangles, and octagons) into a bag. Have each group pull out a shape card. The group must include this shape as part of the kite's overall shape, not just as decoration.

Kite Materials Price List

Plain paper	2¢ per sheet
Construction paper	3¢ per sheet
Tissue paper	2¢ per foot
Waxed paper	2¢ per foot
Aluminum foil	5¢ each
Plastic trash bag	1¢ each
Lunch-size paper bags	2¢ each
Craft sticks	1¢ each
Straws	5¢ each
Wood dowels	5¢ each
Skewers	2¢ per foot
Masking tape	3¢ per foot
Clear tape	2¢ per foot
String for building kite	2¢ per sheet

String for flying the kite is free.

Names

_____

_____

_____

_____

Kite Observations

Color each bar to the highest height reached in that test.

	Test 1	Test 2	Test 3	Test 4
> 5 feet				
5 feet				
4 feet				
3 feet				
2 feet				
1 foot				
< 1 foot				

Write initials in boxes.

Names _____

_____

_____

_____

Kite Test Results

❶ What was the highest the kite flew? _____

....

❷ What was the lowest the kite flew? _____

....

❸ The kite mostly flew at _____ feet.

....

❹ One idea for making our kite better is

_____

Name _____

Kite Checklist

On a scale of 1 to 5, rate yourself.

❶ My collaboration was

1	2	3	4	5
Not good	Okay	Good	Very good	Excellent

One example of good collaboration was when

_____

· ·

❷ My time management was

1	2	3	4	5
Not good	Okay	Good	Very good	Excellent

One example of my good time management was

_____

· ·

❸ My use of materials was

1	2	3	4	5
Not good	Okay	Good	Very good	Excellent

One example of how I used materials well was when

_____

Engineering Butterfly Habitats

Criteria for Product

- Must have a place to store food
- Must keep caterpillars and butterflies from escaping
- Must have a place for caterpillars to hang and spin chrysalises
- Must have enough space for butterflies to fly once they hatch
- Must be easy to release butterflies once they are ready

Constraints for Challenge

- May use only the materials provided
- Must stay within budget of 25¢
- Must complete each stage of the process within its time limit

Challenge

Butterflies arrive in spring! As students prepare to raise butterflies from caterpillars, they design and build habitats to support each stage of the insects' life cycle.

Materials

Habitat Materials (for class)

- Cardboard boxes
- Cardboard pieces
- 50-ft. roll of plastic wrap or cellophane
- 1 roll of aluminum foil
- 12 yd. of tulle fabric, at least 36 in. wide
- Modeling clay, 1½-in. balls
- Jar lids
- Twigs, about 12–14 in. long
- Mud
- Clear tape
- Masking tape
- Yarn or string
- Rubber bands

Note: *Unless quantities are noted, provide an assortment of each item in quantities that are readily available.*

Tools

- Scissors
- Hole punches

Additional Materials

- Markers
- Job cards (page 10)
- Plain paper
- Pencils
- Rulers (cm/mm)
- Bags for packaging mud and twigs
- Sugar water
- Leaves for caterpillar food
- Pennies, 25 per group
- Envelopes or bags for packaging pennies
- Digital camera
- Document camera
- Digital timer

Before You Begin

- Study the butterfly life cycle as part of the regular curriculum.
- Order caterpillars from a school science supplier. Consult supplier information to determine what, if any, food materials to gather, and to confirm that the butterflies may be released outdoors in your area.
- Make a copy of the Observations (page 112) and Test Results (page 113) for each group.
- Make copies of the Price List (page 111) and Checklist (page 114) for each student.
- Make a set of job cards (page 10) for each group.
- Roll modeling clay into balls about 1½ inches in diameter.
- Divide mud and twigs into separate bags.
- Place habitat materials on a table. Make a sign for the price of each material, if desired.
- For each group, place 25 pennies in an envelope or bag.
- Display the Criteria for Product and Constraints for Challenge where students can see them.

5-Step Process

1 ▶ Investigate
45 minutes

- After learning about butterfly life cycles, ask students to think about the habitats of butterflies and what caterpillars and butterflies need to thrive.
- Tell students that they will take on a very important challenge: designing a habitat for caterpillars that will grow into butterflies. In this challenge, living things will depend on the students' engineering skills. Ask students:

  What do living things need to thrive?

  What do these insects need as caterpillars (larvas)?

  How do the insects' needs change when they become chrysalises (pupas)?

  What could you add to the habitat for the butterflies (adults)?

  How can you keep the caterpillars and butterflies from escaping?

  How could you use each of the materials on the table?

- Allow students to touch and examine the materials so they have hands-on information to use in their decision making.
- Review with students the Criteria for Product and Constraints for Challenge, as well as the time limits for Brainstorm, Plan, and Build.

2 ▶ Brainstorm
15 minutes

- Tell students they will work by themselves to brainstorm designs for a butterfly habitat.
- Give each student a copy of the price list and a sheet of plain paper. Have them fold the plain paper to make four boxes. Their task is to draw four designs—one in each section of the paper—for a butterfly habitat. Instruct students to work by themselves silently for 10 minutes.

- Circulate and talk with your students. Ask guiding questions that encourage students to access and apply prior knowledge of natural habitats. Suggested questions:

    How will the caterpillars get their food in your design?

    Why is that material better than another?

    Do the materials cost 25 cents or less, total?

    How will you release the butterflies when they are ready?

3 ▸ Plan
30 minutes

- By now, your students are familiar with the four jobs described on page 7. Invite students to choose one of the four jobs. Tell them to have a second-choice job in mind, too.
- Help students form groups so that each group has one person to do each job.
- Once students are in groups, set the timer for 25 minutes. Instruct students to take turns sharing ideas from Brainstorm. Remind them to weigh the pros and cons of each design in order to come up with a plan they all agree upon.
- Go around the room, listening to conversations and encouraging students to use good collaborative skills.
- Explain that each group member should draw the group's plan. As the group makes final decisions, each student will add the new piece to his copy of the design.
- Be sure that each student adds up the total cost of the habitat and that the cost is within the 25-cent budget. Students should show their work.
- Walk around the room, listening in, prompting students to expand their thinking. Ask questions that guide students to make decisions based on what they have learned in science lessons. Sample questions:

    Will the caterpillars be safe in your habitat? Will they still be safe as butterflies?

    Have you included everything a caterpillar and butterfly need to thrive?

    What do you know about living things that has helped you with this plan?

    Where will the caterpillars (larvas) spin their chrysalises (pupas)?

    Will the habitat keep them from getting too hot, too cold, and too dry?

4 ► Build

45 minutes

- Let the students know it's time to build the butterfly habitats. Set the timer for 45 minutes.
- Give an envelope with 25 cents to each Materials Manager. Invite the Materials Managers to purchase supplies.
- Spend some time with each group. Ask students to tell you what their building procedure is, and to explain what they will do if it turns out their plan isn't working. Correct any misconceptions. Ask guiding questions to encourage cooperative behaviors and empower students to make decisions. Sample questions:

    How is everyone involved in building?

    Are you working on different parts and then coming together, or are you all working on the same part at the same time? (Either approach is fine.)

    Since you can't test your design during the build, how do you know it will work?

    What was your thinking when you designed this part?

    What problems have you had? How did you solve them?

- Make sure that everyone knows the responsibilities of their jobs. Make sure all students perform their collaborative jobs and help build their group's habitat.
- Have students wash hands thoroughly after handling mud, sticks, and other natural materials.
- Have each group put their names on their finished habitats. Place habitats in a safe place.
- When the caterpillars arrive, place a few in each habitat. Give the Recorder in each group an Observation sheet. Give student groups 10 minutes to observe the caterpillars in their habitats and record their observations.
- For caterpillar length, have students use a ruler to estimate the length of one caterpillar that is against the wall of the habitat or is otherwise easy to measure. It is not necessary to take an average of all caterpillar lengths.
- Have students observe every other day for two weeks or until the butterflies emerge from the chrysalises. Each observation period will take about 5 minutes.
- Once the butterflies hatch, feed them sugar water in a jar lid or other shallow container. Allow a few days for them to grow strong. If you plan to have students release the butterflies, wait until the insects are flying around easily in the habitat. Bring cameras outdoors and take pictures as students release the butterflies.

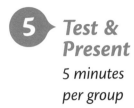

5 ▶ Test & Present

5 minutes per group

- Provide each group with a Test Results page and allow time for students to complete it.
- Tell groups that they each have 5 minutes to present.
- Help the Recorder set up the group's Observations page under the document camera.
- Ask the Speaker to discuss the results of their Observations. Then the Recorder should replace the observations with a picture of the butterflies being released, for the Speaker to talk about.
- Invite students to ask questions about the group's butterfly habitat design or their building process.
- Distribute a Checklist for each student to complete, after all groups have presented.

Opportunities for Differentiation

To make it simpler: Remove the budget constraint. Or, provide each group with a materials kit that includes items needed to build one kind of butterfly habitat. For example, with tulle, rubber bands, and cardboard cut into circles, students could create a wrapped tulle habitat using cardboard as the ceiling and floor. With some additional materials for food and a place for chrysalises to hang, students have a working habitat.

To make it harder: Remove cardboard boxes from the materials. Require the habitat to be freestanding, rather than hanging. This will require students to build the habitat mostly of tulle, but figure out ways to support it.

Butterfly Habitat Materials Price List

Cardboard boxes	10¢ per box
Cardboard pieces	2¢ per piece
Plastic wrap	2¢ per foot
Foil	2¢ per foot
Tulle fabric	4¢ per foot
Masking tape	2¢ per foot
Clear tape	3¢ per foot
Clay	2¢ per ball
String	2¢ per foot
Yarn	2¢ per foot
Rubber bands	1¢ each
Mud	2¢ per bag
Twigs	2¢ per bag
Jar lids	5¢ each

Names _____

_____

_____

_____

Butterfly Habitat Observations

Observation session	1	2	3	4	5	6	7
Date							
Number of caterpillars							
Length of caterpillar (mm)							
Number of chrysalises							
Number of butterflies							

Names _____

_____

_____

_____

Butterfly Habitat Test Results

1 How many caterpillars did not turn into butterflies? _____

2 How big were the caterpillars right before they spun chrysalises? _____

3 How many days did it take for all the chrysalises to hatch? _____

4 Did the habitat keep the insects from escaping?

Yes   No

5 Did the habitat have everything the insects needed?

Yes   Mostly   Not really

6 Was your habitat easy to open and close?

Yes   Mostly   Not really

Butterfly Habitat Checklist

On a scale of 1 to 5, rate yourself.

❶ My collaboration was

1	2	3	4	5
Not good	Okay	Good	Very good	Excellent

One example of good collaboration was when

_____

❷ My time management was

1	2	3	4	5
Not good	Okay	Good	Very good	Excellent

One example of my good time management was

_____

❸ My understanding of life cycles is

1	2	3	4	5
Not good	Okay	Good	Very good	Excellent

I showed my understanding of life cycles when

_____

Engineering
April Shower Umbrellas

Criteria for Product
• To be determined by students during Investigate

Constraints for Challenge
• May use only the materials provided in the kit, but may barter with other groups to get more of the same materials
• Must stay within time limits for each stage of the process

> ### Challenge
> April showers make people wet! Students design and build umbrellas to tackle this problem.

Materials

Umbrella Materials (for each group)
• 8 straws
• 3 plastic shopping bags
• 2 ft. of waxed paper
• 2 pieces of felt (9 in. x 12 in.)
• 10 craft sticks
• 2 ft. of aluminum foil
• 12 coffee stirrers
• 1 foam tray
• 1 yd. of string or yarn
• 2 paper towel tubes
• 4 bath tissue tubes
• 1 yd. of masking tape
• 4 paper plates
• 1 shopping bag (paper or plastic)

Tools
• Tape measures
• Scissors

Additional Materials
• Examples of umbrellas
• 1 stuffed animal toy per group
• Chart paper
• Markers
• Pencils
• Plain paper
• Job cards (page 10)
• Digital timer
• Plastic tub at least 2 ft. wide
• Small plastic container
• Watering can and water
• Digital video cameras (optional)

Before You Begin

- Collect a variety of umbrellas and invite students to bring in more.
- Set out the plastic tub. Place the plastic container upside-down in the tub as a "seat" for the stuffed animals while the umbrellas are tested.
- Assemble a materials kit for each group, following the umbrella materials list. Place all materials in a shopping bag.
- Figure out how many groups of four are in your class. Prepare slips of paper with numbers 1, 2, 3, and so on, so that one number is on each slip of paper and there is one number for each student. Allow for one or more groups of three as needed. Place the numbers in bag.
- Make a set of job cards (page 10) for each group.
- Make a copy of the Product Information sheet (page 120) for each group.
- Make a copy of the Checklist (page 121) for each student.

5-Step Process

1 ▶ Investigate
45 minutes

- Gather students together in a circle. Place the sample umbrellas in the center.
- Invite students to think of different ways to sort the umbrellas. At first, they may focus on properties such as color and size. Encourage them to think about functional properties, such as "the pole pulls in or it doesn't pull in," or "the umbrella is long or short when it's folded."
- Ask questions to help students consider how each property affects the umbrella's usefulness. Guide students to recognize that, while most umbrellas open and close, this is not the property that makes the umbrella do its job. A wide top helps keep water off whatever is under the umbrella. Ask students:

  What is the purpose of an umbrella?

  Can any of these umbrellas do something that another can't?

  Do these umbrellas do anything that doesn't help keep you dry? Why do you think they do that?

  Which umbrella would keep more people dry? Why?

- Show students the stuffed animals. Tell the students that they will design and build umbrellas to protect the animals from April showers. Show them the tub and demonstrate how a stuffed animal will "sit" on the plastic container. The umbrella will be over the animal, and water will be poured on the umbrella.
- Invite students to offer ideas about the Criteria for Product for the umbrellas. Ask students to think about what makes an umbrella work properly, and what makes it fail. Ask students:

  What does an umbrella need to do?

  How will you know whether the umbrella works?

Should the umbrella stand by itself?

Does the umbrella need to fold? Does it need to look pretty?

- As each criterion is agreed upon, add it to a list that is displayed where students can see it. Guide students to avoid criteria that may be unnecessary and difficult, such as having the stuffed animal hold up the umbrella. Unless you are sure you can test outdoors, you may wish to add the criterion that the water from the umbrella must land in the plastic tub.

- Show students the materials in the kit. Ask students:

  What properties do these materials have that might work in an umbrella?

  Does it matter what the top part of the umbrella is made of?

  What are some questions you have about the challenge?

- Review with students the time limits for Brainstorm, Plan, and Build.

2 Brainstorm
35 minutes

- Invite students to choose a number out of the bag, then find the other students with that number to form their group.

- Instruct the students to decide who will take each job. Hand out job cards to each group. Review the responsibilities of each job (page 7).

- Give each group a blank sheet of chart paper and markers. Ask them to work together to think of as many ideas as they can for the design of an umbrella. Set the timer for 20 minutes. Students should talk as they brainstorm, putting all the ideas on paper.

- Remind students that brainstorming is not a time to judge the ideas, but a time to write everything down, then come up with more ideas. Later, they will think about the ideas.

- Observe students as they work. Note good collaborative efforts and creativity. Ask questions to assist them in thinking "outside the box." Suggested questions:

  What material(s) from the kit have you thought about for the top?

  Are there any materials that might not be good for the top? Why?

  How does your design meet the Criteria for Product that the class decided on?

  What are some different ways the umbrella could stay up?

3 Plan
30 minutes

- Tell students it is now time to think about all their ideas. Set the timer for 30 minutes.

- As a group, students decide if there is one idea that they can use or if they need to mix and match.

- Let students know that each group member is expected to draw the plan. All plans within a group should match. If they don't, then the group needs to discuss the plan some more.

- Be sure that the following items are included in each plan: a color-coded sketch, labels that describe materials, and a key explaining which color stands for each material.

- While checking on the plans, ask questions to clarify the students' thinking. Sample questions:

    Why did you decide to design it that way?

    Is this one of your brainstorm ideas or did you mix ideas together?

    Why did you choose that material for the top part?

    Are there any other materials in the kit that would work, if you can't trade for more of that one?

- Allow Speakers to check in with other groups to plan trades if needed. Remind them that it's better to plan ahead for a trade than to start building and find out that no group can trade the materials you need.

4 ▶ Build
40 minutes

- Let the students know it's time to build the umbrellas. Set the timer for 40 minutes.
- Have each group send the Materials Manager to pick up the materials kit.
- Remind the Speakers to make any trades they arranged.
- Ask students to describe the building procedure. If they do not mention the rules for changing the design, remind them that the Speaker must tell you about any changes and explain the reason for them. If the change is approved, they need to update the plan accordingly.
- While walking the room and checking in with groups, be sure that all students are involved in the build and performing their group jobs, as well.
- Talk with the students and ask guiding questions. Sample questions:

    How is each person helping to build the umbrella?

    What techniques are you using to fasten the parts together?

    Did you need to trade for materials? If so, what did you need and what did you trade for it?

    What is the most challenging part of this build?

- As groups finish building, give each Recorder a Product Information sheet. Have them involve the group in completing it.
- Place finished umbrellas in a safe place until it is time to test.

5 ▶ Test & Present
Prepare:
15 minutes;
Test & Present:
10 minutes
per group

- Tell students that when engineers create a new product, the final step is to market it. Marketing means telling people about your product. One way to market a product is through a commercial.
- Give students 15 minutes to prepare and practice a 1-minute commercial for their umbrella. If desired, provide a digital video camera for them to record the commercial. Alternatively, students may perform commercials as part of presenting.
- If students have made videos of their commercials, show these before going outdoors.
- When you are ready to test, fill the watering can. Lead students outdoors to the testing site, and set up the tub with the plastic container seat for the toy, or set up the test indoors. (The seat keeps the toy from getting wet from runoff.)

- Call groups up one at a time. Have them perform their commercial, as appropriate, then set the stuffed animal on the seat in the tub and set up their umbrella over it.
- To test the umbrella, pour water from the watering can over the umbrella. Then stop watering and check the stuffed toy to see if it's still dry.
- Allow 2 minutes for comments and questions from the teacher and students, after each test.
- After all groups have presented, have each student complete a Checklist.

Opportunities for Differentiation

To make it simpler: Supply each group with a shower curtain liner (may be purchased at most dollar stores) in place of the aluminum foil, waxed paper, plastic bags, and felt. Show students how to draw and cut out a large circle for the top of the umbrella. Students then need to decide the umbrella's size, its handle, and the spokes or other support for the plastic circle.

To make it harder: Add to the Criteria for Product the requirement that the umbrella must open and close.

Names _____

_____

_____

_____

April Shower Umbrella Product Information

❶ How many inches across is the umbrella top? _____ inches

❷ How many inches tall is the umbrella? _____ inches

❸ How does the umbrella stay in place?

_____

❹ What is the top of the umbrella made of?

_____

❺ What other features does this umbrella have?

_____

_____

❻ Does the umbrella keep the test subject dry? _____

Name _____

April Shower Umbrella Checklist

On a scale of 1 to 5, rate how well you worked.

❶ My collaboration was

1	2	3	4	5
Not good	Okay	Good	Very good	Excellent

One example of good collaboration was when

_____

❷ My time management was

1	2	3	4	5
Not good	Okay	Good	Very good	Excellent

One example of my good time management is

_____

❸ My ability to come up with ideas was

1	2	3	4	5
Not good	Okay	Good	Very good	Excellent

One example of an idea I came up with was

_____

Engineering Nests

Criteria for Product

Guide students to include the following on the list they come up with during Investigate:

- Must hold together on its own
- Must be large enough and strong enough to hold three eggs and a toy bird
- Must sit on a branch without falling while holding the eggs and the bird

Constraints for Challenge

- May use only materials that birds would use
- Must complete each stage of the process within the time limit

Challenge

Birds are natural engineers, building nests for their eggs in spring. Students learn about biomimicry engineering as they imitate birds by designing and building nests.

Materials

Nest Materials (for class)

- Straw or hay
- Dried grass
- Dried moss
- Twigs
- Leaves
- 2 bags of feathers
- 2 pts. of mud
- 1–2 rolls of string or yarn
- A few paper bags
- Newspapers

Additional Materials

- Computer with projector
- Document camera (optional)
- Video camera (optional)
- Pencils
- Plain paper
- Digital timer
- Job cards (page 10)
- 3 hard-boiled eggs
- Stuffed toy bird
- Sturdy forked branch
- Tape measure

Note: *See Before You Begin. Gather a grocery bag full of each item unless otherwise noted.*

Before You Begin

- Study habitats and life cycles as part of your curriculum.
- Locate images of wild bird nests online. A good source is About.com; on that site, search for "gallery of wild bird nests." Also, if you have bird nests that you have previously collected, bring them in. Check your state's guidelines before collecting any wild animal material, and avoid collecting nests during breeding season.
- Acquire nest-building materials from outdoors (or wait until Plan to do so with your students). If your school has concerns about students handling natural materials, or if there are items you cannot find, most can be purchased at a craft store.
- Locate a suitable branch for testing on the school grounds, if possible. The branch should be low hanging and have a fork or crotch where completed nests may be placed. If a suitable branch is not available, bring in one that you can hold horizontally, or improvise using a long-handled tool such as a barbecue spatula.
- Hard-boil half a dozen chicken eggs for testing (make extras in case of cracking).
- Make a copy of Nest Test Results (page 127) for each group.
- Make a copy of the Nest Checklist (page 128) for each student.

5-Step Process

1 ▶ Investigate
45 minutes

- Introduce the term *biomimicry engineering*. Tell students that *bio* means life and *mimicry* means to copy what something else is doing. Biomimicry engineering happens when humans use ideas from nature to design and build something.
- Show students the real bird nests, if available, and pictures of bird nests. Ask students:

    What materials did birds use to make these nests?
    Where did the birds build the nests?
    Did the birds do anything to make the nest materials hold together?

- Show students three chicken eggs. Explain that many birds that lay eggs this large do not nest in trees. However, the students' engineering task is to design and build a nest that sits in a tree and holds eggs this size.
- Explain that the class first needs to come up with the list of Criteria for Product. Have students examine the nests and photos again. Guide students to come up with a list of properties that add up to a successful nest. Write the list of criteria where students can see it. Ask students:

    How many eggs should the nest hold?
    How long (time) does the nest need to hold together?
    How do birds keep eggs warm? Should the nest hold an adult bird, too?

Where does the nest need to sit?

How strong does the nest need to be? How large?

What questions do you have about the challenge?

- Guide students to be specific, steering them toward ideas that can be implemented and away from those that cannot. As a class, review and revise the list until the class has a short, workable Criteria for Product list.
- Review with students the Constraints for Challenge and the time limits for Brainstorm, Plan, and Build.

2 ▶ Brainstorm
35 minutes

- Invite students to choose a job that they would like to do for this challenge: Recorder, Timekeeper, Speaker, or Materials Manager.
- Once students have chosen jobs, assist them in forming groups of four so that each group has someone to do each job. If there are any groups of three, then one student takes two jobs.
- Give each group a blank sheet of paper. Ask them to work together to think of materials they need to build a nest. Set the timer for 20 minutes of brainstorm time.
- Walk around and listen to conversations. Remind students to be respectful of each other as they talk about nesting materials. Ask questions that remind them to think about real nests. Suggested questions:

    What did you notice about the real nests we looked at?

    Are all the materials on your list things that a bird could find?

    What could you use to hold the nest together?

- The Recorder writes down the list as students decide on materials.
- After 20 minutes, ask the Speakers to read their groups' lists to the class.
- As each group takes turns calling out materials, create a class list for all students to see. Guide students toward the list provided on page 122.
- Collect the needed nest materials from storage. (Do not let students know that you were prepared with your own list ahead of time.) Display them on a table. Or, if time permits, allow students to help collect dried grass, twigs, and leaves from outside. Avoid grass clippings from lawns and fields that have had chemicals applied.
- Place all nest materials on a table for students to see.

3 ▶ Plan
30 minutes

- Instruct students to work together to design a nest, using only the materials on the table. Explain that they will use only their hands to build the nest. Birds do not use tools and so, neither will they. Set the timer for 30 minutes.
- Check in with each group. Join in on conversations. Ask questions, but do not offer suggestions.
- As you view plans, ask questions to help students make smart decisions. Sample questions:

    How can you be sure the eggs won't roll out?

    Will the nest be strong enough with those materials?

How many inches across will the nest be? How many inches around?

Will the nest rest on the tree branch? How do you know?

What do you know about where birds build their nests that has helped you with this plan?

- Tell the class that each student will draw a picture of the plan that the whole group agrees to. All plans within a group must match. If they do not, students need to discuss the differences and agree on one design. Remind students to label all plans with the materials to use.

4 Build
40 minutes

- Let the students know it's time to build the nests. Remind them that they have no tools, only their hands. Set the timer for 40 minutes.
- Have each group send the Materials Manager to the table to pick up needed materials.
- Ask students to explain the process rules for building a product, including an explanation of what to do if they need to change the plan. Correct any misconceptions about the process.
- As you circulate, check that all students are building the nest and doing their group jobs.
- Visit each group and talk with the students as they build. Ask guiding questions to keep students on task. Sample questions:

What is each person doing to help build the nest?

What are you doing to turn large materials like newspaper into smaller pieces that a bird could manage?

How are you checking to see if your nest meets the Criteria for Product?

What is the most challenging part of making the nest?

- Place finished nests in a safe place until it is time to test.

5 Test & Present
10 minutes per group

- Call on one group at a time to present.
- If you go outdoors bring all nests and eggs, the toy bird, and the timer.
- Give the Recorder a copy of the Nest Test Results page to write down results.
- Invite the group to talk briefly about their nests. Presentations should include information about why they chose specific materials, how they changed the size and shape of materials, and how the materials are held together.
- Hand the Materials Manager a tape measure. As needed, explain how to measure the nest across the middle (diameter) and all the way around (circumference).
- Instruct the Materials Manager to place the nest on the test branch.
- Allow the nest to sit for 30 seconds (or the duration listed in the Criteria) to be sure it stays in place and holds together. The Timekeeper may use the timer to check it.

- If the nest stays on the branch, place one egg in it. If the nest holds, place the second egg, then the third. If the nest holds all 3 eggs and it's still okay, place the toy bird in the nest.

- Instruct the Materials Manager to remove everything from the nest and take the nest off the branch. Then explain that their group isn't done yet. Engineers don't test only one time; they repeat the test. That way they know their product can hold up.

- Follow the same procedure to test the nest again and record the data.

- Invite students to ask questions about the design or the process.

- When testing and presenting are completed, provide each student with a copy of the Checklist to complete.

Opportunities for Differentiation

To make it simpler: Provide the list of materials to students, rather than allowing them to develop it themselves. Demonstrate different ways to work with the materials, such as ripping, shredding, braiding, and weaving. Give students a base, such as a small paper plate, to place inside the nest to stabilize and strengthen it.

To make it harder: Tell students they must incorporate all of the materials on their original list into the nest and that each material must serve a purpose, not just serve as decoration. Or increase the number of eggs the nest must hold.

Names _____ _____

_____ _____

Nest Test Results

	Test 1	Test 2
Time on branch	_____ min.	_____ min.
How many eggs?		
Held adult bird?		

❶ How many inches across is the nest? _____ inches

....

❷ How many inches around is the nest? _____ inches

....

❸ Did any part of the nest break? _____
Which part? _____

....

❹ What could you do to improve this nest?

_____

_____

Name _____

Nest Checklist

Rate how well you worked.

❶ I kept trying when things did not go as planned.

1	2	3
Yes	Sort of	Not really

One example of how I did this is

_____

❷ I used ideas from real nests in the nest design.

1	2	3
Yes	Sort of	Not really

One idea I used is

_____

❸ I used only my hands to build the nest.

1	2	3
Yes	Sort of	Not really

❹ I did my job for the group.

1	2	3
Yes	Sort of	Not really

Engineering
May Flower Watering Systems

Criteria for Product

To be determined by students. Suggested list:
- Must water all four cups in the group at once
- Must water plants slowly over several days after one refill
- Must keep the soil damp, not dry or soaking wet

Constraints for Challenge

- May use only the materials provided
- Must stay within $1.00 budget
- Each stage of the design process must be completed within its time limit

Challenge

"April showers bring May flowers." Since April showers don't fall indoors, students design and build indoor watering systems for their May flowers.

Materials

Watering System Materials (for the class)

- Assorted plastic bottles
- Plastic food-service gloves
- Plastic or foam egg cartons
- 20 foam cups
- Cardboard boxes, sturdy
- Foam trays
- 1 large bag fish tank gravel
- Paper towels
- Sponges (new)
- 12–15 PVC pipes, 2-ft. lengths
- 12–15 PVC pipes, 1-ft. lengths
- 12 or more PVC pipe connectors
- 1 roll of aluminum foil
- 1 roll of plastic wrap
- 1 ball of sturdy string
- 2 doz. clothespins
- Masking tape
- Duct tape

Additional Materials

- Chart paper
- Markers
- Pencils
- Plain paper
- Digital timer
- Job cards (page 10)
- 1 bag of potting soil
- 1 packet of marigold seeds
- 2–3 doz. paper cups
- Coins (pennies, nickels, dimes), $1.00 per group
- Envelopes or bags to hold coins

Tools

- Scissors
- Hole punches
- Staplers
- Pen knife (teacher use only)
- Glue gun (teacher use only)

Note: *Unless a quantity is specified, gather items in quantities that are readily available.*

Before You Begin

- Study plants as part of your regular curriculum.

- A week ahead of this challenge, prepare one paper cup for each student. Fill each cup with soil and label it with the student's name. Prepare a few extras as well. Have students plant marigold seeds in their cups. Plant the extra cups yourself. Keep the soil damp until the seeds sprout.

- Purchase PVC pipes and connectors. Most hardware and home-supply stores will cut pipes to length for you. Any diameter pipe will work, but be sure to purchase matching connectors.

- For each group, prepare an envelope or bag with $1.00 in loose change. Use coins that your students can easily recognize and work with. For example, if they do not yet know coin values, put 100 pennies in each bag. If they do know coin values, use a mix of pennies, nickels, dimes, and possibly quarters.

- Make up about 10 bags of gravel, using about ¼ cup per bag.

- Place all watering system materials and tools on a table.

- Make a copy of the Price List (page 134), Observations (page 135), and Test Results (page 136) for each group.

- Make a copy of the Checklist (page 137) for each student.

5-Step Process

 **1 Investigate**
45 minutes

- Have students check on their marigold plants. When they've returned to their seats, ask if they remember all the things plants need. Make a list of their answers. (A possible list might include light, soil, water, space, air; your curriculum's list may vary slightly.)

- Refer to the list. Ask students where they should place their marigold cups to help the plants grow now that they've sprouted (for example, near a window where they can get light). As a class, discuss how the plants will get the other things on the list if they're placed in this location.

- Discuss the idea of giving water to the plants. Explain that there may be times when students cannot water the plants, such as weekends and very busy school days. Tell them that they have a new engineering challenge: Design and build an indoor watering system that will give "April showers" water to their "May flowers."

- Invite students to offer ideas about the Criteria for Product for this challenge. Keep a list of agreed-upon criteria where students can see it. Guide students toward the criteria listed at the start of the challenge.

- Ask questions to get students thinking about how they could set up a watering system so they can add water only once, but the system waters the plants over several days. Ask students:

  What could you use to hold a large amount of water?

Where in the system should the water be placed, so it can water the plants?

How could you slow down the flow of the water so it doesn't drain out all at once?

How could you hold the watering system in place?

How will you know if your watering system is successful?

- Show students the watering system materials on the table. Ask students:

   How are these materials alike? How are they different?

   What properties do these materials have that might help build a watering system?

   What could you use this item for? How about this one?

   What questions do you have about the challenge?

- Let students know that they will be allowed to use only the materials on the table and that they will have a budget of $1.00 to spend.

- Review the class's Criteria for Product list, as well as the Constraints for Challenge. Point out the time limits for Brainstorm, Plan, and Build.

2 Brainstorm
30 minutes

- Tell students that they'll be thinking up as many ideas as they can for the design of a system that can slowly water four plant cups at the same time.

- Remind students that Brainstorm is a time to let the ideas flow. They need to get all of their ideas down on paper without stopping to think which ones they like best. Remind them to label their drawings to show the materials they plan to use.

- Give each student a blank sheet of paper. Allow 15 minutes for brainstorming.

- Peek over students' shoulders to check their progress as they work. Guide students to use their science knowledge as they design. Suggested questions:

   What are you using to slow down the water flow?

   Will the plant get watered all over or only in one place?

   How will the watering system stay in place?

   How will you fill the system?

- After 15 minutes have passed, give students a second sheet of paper. Tell them they have 10 minutes to decide which idea is their favorite, and to draw and label it again neatly. Let them know that it's okay to make minor changes to their design if they like.

3 Plan
45 minutes

- Tell students that they will form groups based on their designs.

- Give students 5 minutes to walk around the room with the sketches of their favorite ideas. They need to look at each other's sketches and talk about them, so they can find people who have designs similar to their own. Once they have three or four people in the group, they should sit down together.

- Visit each group as they sit down. Assign each student in the group the job she would be least likely to choose (Timekeeper, Recorder, Speaker, Materials Manager). Let students know that you assigned those jobs to help stretch them in new directions.

• Provide each group with a price list for the materials, a sheet of chart paper, and markers.

• Point out the prices for Tool Rental. Explain that the 5-minute tool rental charge applies even if they use a tool for only one minute. They're also charged for the extra time if they forget to return a tool. So they should think about all the things they need each tool for, how many times they'll need each tool, and for how long. Then they should include those costs in their plans.

• Introduce yourself as the Contractor. You will be available for hire during the Build. Groups can hire you to do the jobs listed, as well as any other job they cannot do themselves. Groups need to include contractor costs in their plans.

• Tell students to use their brainstormed ideas to come up with one group plan. Each plan needs the following items: a description of how the system works; a sketch with labels showing materials; a materials list; and the total cost to build the system, including the cost of materials, tool rentals, and contractor hires.

• Set the timer to give students 30 minutes to plan. Visit groups as they work. Guide them to draw up detailed plans. Suggested questions to ask:

> *Can you explain how this system will work?*
>
> *How do you know the system is big enough to water all four cups?*
>
> *What holds the water? What holds up the thing that holds the water?*
>
> *How will you keep the water from pouring out all at once?*
>
> *Did everyone have a voice in this plan? Were everyone's suggestions considered?*

4 ▶ Build
45 minutes

• Let the students know it's time to build the watering systems.

• Call on student volunteers to review the building procedure, as well as the responsibilities of each group job. Be sure students mention the procedure for revising plans: everyone agrees, the teacher is asked for approval, and the plans are revised. These tasks are the responsibilities of the Speaker and Recorder.

• Set the timer for 40 minutes and point it out to the Timekeepers.

• Give each Materials Manager $1.00. Serve as the Shopkeeper as they purchase materials. When all groups have their materials, switch from Shopkeeper to Contractor.

• Check in regularly with each group between your Contractor jobs. If groups are stuck, do not offer suggestions. Rather, ask questions to guide students to work through challenges and misconceptions. Sample questions:

How have you divided the work so that everyone has a part and you complete the task on time?

What are the steps to make the watering system work? Let's think about each step.

What holds up the container of water? Will it hold the container when it's full? How can you test it?

- As groups finish, help them set up their systems for long-term use. (This does not count as a Contractor hire.) Give each Recorder an Observations page, and instruct them to fill in the first observation.
- Every 3 to 4 days, remind students to check on their May flowers and to note observations on the sheet. Remind them to add water to their watering systems as needed.
- Continue checking plants for 2 to 3 weeks.

⑤ Test & Present

5 minutes per group

- Give each group a Test Results page and provide time to complete it.
- Call on groups one at a time. Have each group gather around its watering system to present.
- Ask students to say how much their water system cost and how it works, and to describe any changes they had to make to their system. Then ask them to describe their observations.
- Allow 2 minutes per group for additional questions and comments from the teacher and students.
- When all groups have completed their presentations, distribute copies of the Checklist to each student.

Opportunities for Differentiation

To make it simpler: Remove the budget constraint. Provide a box or tub to hold the cups, and have students build the watering system around the box.

To make it harder: Tell students that they must design a watering system that will keep the flowers properly watered for 2 to 3 weeks without refilling.

May Flower Watering System Price List

Materials Prices

16-ounce plastic bottle	5¢ each
1-liter plastic bottle	10¢ each
2-liter plastic bottle	15¢ each
Plastic gloves	5¢ each
Egg cartons	2¢ per cup (cut upon request)
Foam coffee cups	5¢ each
Gravel	10¢ per bag
Paper towel	2¢ each
Sponge	7¢ each
Cardboard box	10¢ each
Foam tray	5¢ each
Plastic pipe, 1-foot length	10¢ each
Plastic pipe, 2-foot length	15¢ each
Pipe connectors	5–10¢ each
Foil	5¢ per foot
Plastic wrap	3¢ per foot
String	5¢ per yard
Clothespins	2¢ each
Masking tape	3¢ per yard
Duct tape	5¢ per yard

Tool Rental   (Minimum charge per session is 5 minutes.)

Stapler	10¢ per 5 minutes
Scissors	5¢ per 5 minutes
Hole punch	5¢ per 5 minutes

Contractor Hire   5¢ per job (Ask about other jobs)

- Cut bottles
- Cut boxes
- Cut egg cartons
- Poke holes
- Use glue gun

Names _____

_____

_____

_____

May Flower Watering System Observations

Today's date	Did you refill the water today? (Y/N)	How is the soil today? (dry, damp, wet)	How tall is the plant in inches?

Names _____

_____

_____

_____

May Flower Watering System Test Results

1 How much did your watering system cost to build? _____

....

2 How many times did you need to refill the water? _____

....

3 Did every cup in the group get watered? _____

....

4 Was the soil damp (not wet or dry) most days? _____

....

5 Was your watering system successful? _____

Why or why not?

_____

Name _____

May Flower Watering System Checklist

Rate yourself and your group on a scale of 1 to 5.

❶ I remembered to do my group job.

1	2	3	4	5
No	A little	Sometimes	Mostly	Almost always

❷ My group's time management was

1	2	3	4	5
Poor	Not good	Good	Very good	Excellent

❸ I helped the group figure out what to do when our plan didn't work.

1	2	3	4	5
No	A little	Sometimes	Mostly	Yes

One way that I helped figure out what to do was

_____

_____

Engineering
Farm Fences

Criteria for Product

- Must be 5 feet tall (model is shorter)
- Must be at least 100 feet long (model is shorter)
- Must be in a closed shape (square, rectangle, circle, etc.)
- Must stand up on its own and stay up when animals bump into it
- Must be able to see the animals inside the fenced area
- Must have a way for people to get in
- Must prepare a way to tell farmers about the fence

Constraints for Challenge

- Materials for the model must be found in the classroom
- In the model, 1 large paper clip = 5 feet of fence length (a scale of 1 inch = 2½ feet, though the term scale is not used)
- Paper clips are for measurement, not part of the fence
- Work must be completed within the time limits of each stage of the process

Challenge

Old MacDonald had a farm. And on that farm he had some animals. So Old MacDonald needs a fence to keep the animals from wandering! Students design fences for Old MacDonald, then build models to demonstrate them.

Materials

Fence Materials (for the class)

- Blocks
- Cardboard
- Clothespins
- Construction paper
- Dominoes
- Lego bricks or similar
- Unifix cubes
- Pipe cleaners
- Toothpicks
- Straws
- Craft sticks
- Pencils
- Modeling clay (1-in. balls)
- Clear tape
- Masking tape

Tools (for each group)

- 30 large (2-in.) paper clips
- Bag or envelope to hold paper clips
- Scissors
- Rulers

Additional Materials

- Computer and projector
- Small plastic animals
- Dollhouse furniture
- Job cards (page 10)
- Chart paper
- Markers
- Pencils
- Plain paper

Note: *Items on Fence Materials list are suggestions. Substitutions are allowed, and quantities may be whatever is readily available.*

Before You Begin

- Study farm animals and sing or read "Old MacDonald Had a Farm."
- Invite another adult from the school staff to play the part of Old MacDonald during Test & Present.
- Online, locate examples of different farm fence designs to show students. Good image search terms include "fence" coupled with "farm, ranch, horse, cattle," or "stock." Omit any images of electric fences.
- Place 30 large paper clips in a bag or envelope for each group.
- Make a copy of Product Information (page 143) for each group.
- Make a copy of the Checklist (page 144) for each student.

5-Step Process

 **Investigate**
45 minutes

- Ask students how Old MacDonald can keep his animals from running away. If they do not offer the idea of a fence, guide them until they suggest it.
- If they haven't guessed yet, let them know that they will design a fence.
- Tell students that there are many different designs for fences. Display the images of different fence designs you found.
- Ask students to examine closely the pictures of fences. Have them look for things that all the fences have in common, such as shape and size, as well as things that are different about them, such as materials. Write student observations where everyone can see them.
- Explain that a farm fence is a very large object. Ask students where they can build fences. Guide students to recognize that there isn't enough room in the classroom, then show them the small plastic farm animals and doll furniture. Say that these are *models* of larger objects.
- Explain that when engineers design large objects they build a small model first. Building a model lets them test out ideas and make changes before they've spent the time and money to build a big product. Tell students that they will build a model fence. Old MacDonald can look at the model fences before ordering a life-size fence. But how will he know how big the model fence is compared with the real fence?
- Show students a large paper clip. Tell them that, for their model, each large paper clip stands for 5 feet. (This is a scale of 1 inch = 2½ feet, but do not introduce the term *scale*.)
- Review the size criteria for the model fence. Ask students how many paper clips tall the fence needs to be (5 feet = 1 paper clip). As a class, figure out how many paper clips long to make the fence model. Skip count by 5s and add 1 paper clip, in a chain, for every count of 5. When you reach 100, count up how many paper clips you have (20). So the fence must be at least 20 paper clips long, but it may be longer.

- Tell students it's time to start thinking about their fence models. To design the best possible fence, they need to consider many things. Review the list of observations from the fence photos. Ask students:

    What parts of a fence hold it up?

    What parts of a fence hold the animals in?

    How do the parts of a fence connect?

    How can you be sure a fence will hold the animals in?

    Can the farmer see the animals through the fence?

    How do people and animals get in and out of a fenced-in area?

- Also review the Criteria for Product and Constraints for Challenge, as well as the time limits for Brainstorm, Plan, and Build. Tell students they will have time to prepare a way to tell farmers about the fence during the Test & Present stage.

2 ▶ Brainstorm
20 minutes

- Explain that the class will spend 10 minutes coming up with a list of possible materials. Set the timer for 10 minutes.

- Ask students to think about materials around the classroom. Which materials might work for building a model fence? As students name materials, bring out the ones you have available and place them on a table.

- At the end of 10 minutes, let students investigate the materials on the table. Discuss their properties as a class. Ask students:

    What part of a fence could you use this for?

    Can this item stand up on its own? Which part of the model fence would that help with?

    Is this item tall enough for a fence post in the model? How can you tell?

    What item from the real world could this item stand for?

    What makes this object good for a model fence? Is it the object's shape? Its size? Its flexibility or stiffness?

    What will you use to hold the model fence together?

    Are there enough of these available to make a fence 20 paper clips long?

- Explain to students that for this challenge, they need pictures in their heads of the kind of fence they want to build. They won't draw it yet.

3 ▶ Plan
40 minutes

- Tell students to think about the model fence they want to build. What is it made of? How does it open and close?

- Tell students they will make groups of three or four with other students who have similar ideas. Give them 5 minutes to walk around the room, chatting with each other to find others who share their vision. Once they have enough people in a group, they sit down.

- Visit each group as it sits down. Assign each student in the group the job he would be least likely to choose (Timekeeper, Recorder, Speaker, Materials Manager, as described on page 7). Let students know that you assigned those jobs in order to help them stretch themselves in new directions.

- Provide each group with a sheet of chart paper and a set of markers. Set the timer for 25 minutes.

- Tell students that, for this activity, the whole group should work together to draw one plan. The plan should show how many paper clips (or feet) tall the fence is, and how many paper clips (or feet) long it is. Encourage them to use a different color marker for each material, and to make a key showing what each color means.

- As you go around the room talking with the students, ask questions to extend their thinking and push them to be innovative and creative. Suggested questions:

    How many of those will you need to make the fence model tall enough? To make it long enough?

    Why is that the best material for this part of the model fence?

    What makes this fence design better than another?

    Is it possible to make a fence that does the same job with fewer materials?

    How will that part of the fence stand up?

    Does that design meet all the criteria?

4 Build

45 minutes

- Let the students know it's time to build the model fence. Give them 1 minute to discuss with their groups the responsibilities of each job, the time limits, and the building procedures. Walk around and listen in. Make sure they discuss important points in the process, such as the steps to get approval if a plan must change.

- Answer any questions students have about their jobs, the process, or anything else. Give each Materials Manager a set of paper clips for measuring the fence, and tell them to get whatever materials their group needs.

- Set the timer for 45 minutes. Circulate around the room as students build. Ask questions that help students explain their thinking and choices. Pay attention to good collaboration and praise students for good efforts. Ask questions such as:

    How did you decide who should build each part of the fence?

    How are you measuring the fence?

    What shape is the fenced-in area?

    Where can people get into the fenced-in area? Can animals get out there?

    Have you run into any problems with the fence or with each other? How are you working to solve them?

- Give each group a Product Information sheet. Instruct the Recorder to fill it in.
- Place the model fences and Product Information sheets in a safe place until it is time to present.

5 ▸ Test & Present

20 minutes planning, then 5 minutes per group

- Confirm that Old MacDonald can join your class on the day of the presentations. Prepare Old MacDonald by explaining the Criteria and Constraints, so she knows what to look for when choosing which fence to order, based on the models and advertisements.
- Assign each group a place in the room to set up their model fence. Give each group a few plastic animals to fence in, if desired.
- Tell students that they need to come up with a way to advertise their fence. Remind students that their main customers are farmers. Ask students to think about the best way to reach farmers. A newspaper advertisement? A poster in a store? Something catchy on the radio, like a song or jingle? A television commercial? An email message? They have 20 minutes to come up with anything they need to advertise and explain their fence before Old MacDonald comes shopping. Set the digital timer.
- At the end of 20 minutes, call in Old MacDonald. Bring everyone over to the first presentation area. The first group presents their marketing piece (advertisement, jingle, commercial) to Old MacDonald, then gives the farmer their Product Information sheet to review.
- Continue around the room, letting each group present.
- Ask Old MacDonald to choose one fence to purchase and to give reasons for making that choice, including how well the fence meets the Criteria for Product.

Opportunities for Differentiation

To make it simpler: Before you begin, assemble 30 basic fence pieces, each made with one craft stick glued horizontally across the middle of two craft sticks standing vertically. Provide each group with five or six of these starter pieces. Allow students to work from this design to add to it and improve it.

To make it harder: Challenge students to compete to see which group can use the fewest objects in the model fence, while still meeting all the Criteria for Product.

Names _____   _____

_____   _____

Farm Fence Product Information

1 How tall is the model fence?   _____ paper clips

2 How tall is the real fence?   _____ feet

3 How long is the model fence?   _____ paper clips

4 How long is the real fence?   _____ feet

5 What shape is the fence?   _____

6 What holds the fence up when an animal bumps it?

_____

7 Can the farmer see in?   _____

8 How does the farmer go in and out?

_____

9 Why should a farmer buy this fence instead of another?

_____

Name _____

Farm Fence Checklist

On a scale of 1 to 5, rate yourself. 1 is worst. 5 is best.

❶ For working with others, I rate myself a _____
because _____.

....

❷ For using time, I rate myself a _____
because _____.

....

❸ I helped my group design the fence in this way

_____.

....

On a scale of 1 to 5, rate your group as a whole.

❹ Working Together: _____
I rate our group this way because

_____.

❺ Use of Time: _____
I rate our group this way because

_____.

Engineering
Fish Catchers

Criteria for Product

- Must be waterproof, although water is not part of the test
- Must be easy to use
- Must be easy to carry and travel with
- Must reach the fish from a distance of 2 feet
- Must catch and hold at least three plastic fish. More fish result in a higher score

Constraints for Challenge

- Only materials found in the classroom or brought in for this challenge may be used
- Each group has three attempts to catch fish during Test & Present
- Each design stage must be completed within time limits

Challenge

It's fun to go fishing in summer. Throughout history, humans have invented many tools to catch fish. In this challenge, students design and build their own fish catchers.

Materials

Fish Catcher Materials (for class)

- 6 or more wood dowels, 2–4 ft. long
- 6 or more PVC pipes, 2-ft. lengths
- Sticks from trees
- String
- Yarn
- Twine
- 100 ft. of fishing line
- Paper towel or bath tissue tubes
- Empty soda cans
- 3 yd.+ of fiberglass window screening
- Pipe cleaners
- Wire coat hangers
- Clear tape
- Masking tape

Tools

- Rulers
- Tape measures
- Scissors
- Hole punch

Additional Materials

- Chart paper
- Markers
- Pencils
- Plain paper
- Digital timer
- Job cards (page 10)
- Fishing gear examples (rod, reel, net)
- 24 or more strong magnets
- 10 plastic fish
- 10 large paper clips
- Hula-Hoop (optional)

Note: *Except as noted, provide items in quantities that are readily available.*

Before You Begin

- Complete any lessons on oceans and fish from your curriculum.
- Make a copy of Product Score (page 149) for each group.
- Make a copy of the Checklist (page 150) for each student.
- Collect and bring in samples of fishing gear such as nets, fishing poles, and lures. Do not bring in any fish hooks.
- Place suggested materials in areas where students can see them, but where they are not obviously displayed as materials for the challenge.
- Use tape to attach large paper clips to 10 plastic fish that are each about the same size and weight. Test to make sure that the magnets you're using can pick up the fish. If not, either get stronger magnets or make fish from cardboard instead.

- Build the test setup so students can see it during Investigate. Set the Hula-Hoop in a clear, open area. Place the fish in the middle. Mark a distance of 2 feet from the Hula-Hoop in all directions, using rope or small objects.

5-Step Process

1 ▶ Investigate
60 minutes

- Gather students in a circle on the carpet or around a table. Place the real life fishing tools in the center of the circle.
- Call on students to share what they observe about these tools. Ask questions to encourage observations. For example:

  What does this tool do?
  Which tool helps to reach over a long distance?
  Which tool catches the fish?
  What does the reel do?

  Discuss how students can use their observations in the design of a fish catcher.
- Tell students it's time to design fish catchers. Lead them to the test setup. Explain that, because hooks are too dangerous, they will catch fish with magnets instead. Show them the fish with the paper clips, then explain the parts of the test setup. Students must stand outside of the large circle while using their fish catchers to catch fish inside the Hula-Hoop "pond."
- Review the Criteria for Product and Constraints for Challenge.
- Review the time limits for Brainstorm, Plan, and Build.

2 ▶ Brainstorm
15 minutes

- Tell students that you'll brainstorm as a class. Everyone will be able to see the Brainstorm ideas during Plan.
- Encourage students to look around the classroom for materials they could use. Say that they may bring in other materials for this challenge, but they

cannot bring in actual fishing gear and they must have the permission of adults at home.

- Ask students to think about the parts of a fish catcher, such as handles, line, or netting. How can they build each part using materials available in the classroom? Suggested questions:

    What materials could you use to reach the fish?

    What materials could you use to catch the fish once you reach them?

    How will these materials hold up in water?

- As students list ideas, write them on chart paper or use another method that all students can see.

3 ▶ Plan
30 minutes

- Have students form groups of four in whatever way they choose.
- Once groups are formed, students choose jobs (descriptions on page 7). Any method of choosing is allowed as long as each person has at least one job.
- Provide each group with chart paper, pencils, and markers for sketching out their plan. Set the timer for 20 minutes.
- Tell students that for this challenge, all the students in a group work together on one version of the plan. As they plan, they should include rough measurements, describe how the fish catcher will work, and use a different color to show each different material.
- Walk the room to check on group progress. Remind students of the criteria and ask how their design takes care of each item on the list. Suggested questions:

    How far can your fish catcher reach to catch fish?

    How do you bring the fish back in once they've been caught?

    How many fish does your catcher hold at once?

4 ▶ Build
45 minutes

- Let students know it's time to build the fish catchers. Allow two minutes for groups to review the procedure for Build. Drop in on conversations to be sure students are mentioning all the important steps.
- Circulate around the room, chatting with each group. Lead students to their own conclusions by asking guiding questions, such as:

    What is everyone's job in this group? What is everyone's role in building the fish catcher?

    Are you testing as you go? How many fish has it caught so far?

    Have you had any surprises, or anything that didn't work as planned?

- Place the fish catchers in a safe place until it is time to present.

5 **Test & Present**

15 minutes per group

- Set up the test area again, as you did for Investigate. Call groups one at a time.

- Give a Product Score sheet to the Recorder. Remind the Recorder to write down all scores and results.

- Ask the Speaker to demonstrate the fish catcher without trying to catch fish. The Speaker should explain what the fish catcher is made of, how it works, why the group chose to design it the way they did, and anything else that the group thinks is important. Allow the class to ask questions.

- Decide whether the materials this group used would survive being placed in water. Give the group a score for this requirement, based on the score sheet, and explain the reason for it.

- Invite four students from another group to give the fish catcher a score for how easy it is to use, based on the score sheet.

- Invite four different students to score how easy the fish catcher is to carry and travel with.

- Tell the group they have three tries to catch as many fish from the "pond" as possible. As needed, suggest that the Materials Manager, Timekeeper, and Recorder each have one turn.

- Follow the same procedure for all remaining groups. Discuss and compare results as a class when all groups have finished, then distribute the Checklist sheets to all students.

Opportunities for Differentiation

To make it simpler: Give students a list of basic materials for a fishing pole. Then, rather than scoring the fishing pole, have students list product information about it, such as length, how it works, and so forth.

To make it harder: Increase the distance between the "pond" and where students stand. Add a requirement for the fish catcher to include a pulley of some sort, or to actually work in a large container of water.

Names _____ _____

_____ _____

Fish Catcher Product Score

Requirement	Score

❶ Waterproof
All materials are waterproof = 3 points
Most materials are waterproof = 2 points
One material is waterproof = 1 point
No materials are waterproof = 0 points   _____

❷ Easy to use
Very easy to use = 3 points
Kind of easy to use = 2 points
Not easy to use = 1 point
Breaks when used = 0 points   _____

❸ Easy to carry and travel with
Can fit into a standard backpack = 3 points
Can fit into a large suitcase = 2 points
Easy to carry but very long = 1 point
Difficult to carry or travel with = 0 points   _____

❹ Number of fish caught in 3 tries
(Score 1 point for each fish caught)   _____

Total score   _____

Name _____

Fish Catcher Checklist

On a scale of 1 to 5, rate yourself.

❶ I worked well with others to get the job done.

1	2	3	4	5
Not often	A little	Some	A lot	Almost always

One example is

_____

❷ I made good use of time.

1	2	3	4	5
Not often	A little	Some	A lot	Almost always

I say this because

_____

❸ One thing I did really well was

_____

_____

On a scale of 1 to 5, rate your group as a whole. 1 is low. 5 is high.

❹ Working together: _____

❺ Good use of time: _____

❻ Good use of materials: _____

150 *Engineer Through the Year (Grades K–2) Copymaster © Crystal Springs Books*

Engineering
Waterproof Containers

Criteria for Product

- Must be big enough to hold a sandwich
- Must be easy to put the sandwich in and take it out multiple times
- Must be durable and reusable
- Must float in water
- Must keep sandwich dry for 1 minute (higher scores for up to 5 minutes)

Constraints for Challenge

- Only materials from the kit may be used
- The sandwich cannot be wrapped before it is placed into the container
- Each stage of the design process must be completed within its time limit

Challenge

Summertime means water fun! Water fun means the need to keep some items dry. Students design and build waterproof containers that hold sandwiches at the beach.

Materials

Container Materials (for each group plus extras)

- 3 sandwich bags (tuck-and-fold style)
- 3 ft. of aluminum foil
- 3 ft. of waxed paper
- 2 paper plates
- 1 plastic shopping bag (as a material)
- 1 foam tray
- 5 paper clips
- 5 twist ties
- 1 yd. of masking tape
- 5 pipe cleaners
- 1 shopping bag (paper or plastic, to hold kit)

Tools

- Scissors
- Hole punch

Additional Materials

- Chart paper
- Markers
- Pencils
- Paper
- Digital timer
- Job cards (page 10)
- 1 or more large plastic tubs
- Water
- 12 pennies or other weights
- A few sandwiches

- Towels for cleanup
- Digital video cameras (optional)

Before You Begin

- Assemble a materials kit for each group by placing items from the list in a shopping bag. Make up an extra kit for use during Investigate.
- Make a copy of the Product Score sheet (page 156) for each group.
- Make a copy of the Checklist (page 157) for each student.
- Fill one or more plastic tubs with water for use during Investigate, Build, and Test. Plan to test outdoors if possible.
- Make a few sandwiches to use in Investigate and in Test & Present. Although no one will eat the sandwiches, use ingredients that do not pose an allergy threat.

5-Step Process

1 **Investigate**
45 minutes

- Ask students what kinds of water play they enjoy in the summer: swimming, boating, running in a sprinkler? Do they get hungry while they're playing in the water? Do they like soggy sandwiches? (Probably not!)
- Tell students that they will design and build sandwich containers that are waterproof and that float the sandwich. That way, their lunch won't get soggy or sink and disappear if it falls in the water before they get to eat it.
- Carry an extra materials kit and an extra sandwich over to a water tub. Ask students to gather around.
- Call on student volunteers to test the items in the extra materials kit. Make sure every student can see how each item reacts to being placed in water.
- Challenge students to place weights, such as pennies, on each material to see what happens.
- Let students touch the sandwich to feel its texture and weight. Then place the sandwich into the water to see how it reacts. Let students touch the soggy sandwich again after it's out of the water.
- Ask students to describe how each of the materials reacted in the water. Prompt discussion with questions such as these:

  Which materials sink? Which float?

  Did any of the materials hold up the pennies? Can you make them hold up the pennies by shaping them a certain way?

  Which materials get soggy? Which keep their shape when wet?

  What did the sandwich look like when it came out of the water? What did it feel like?

- Review the Criteria for Product and Constraints for Challenge, as well as the time limits for Brainstorm, Plan, and Build.

2 ▶ Brainstorm
15 minutes

- Set the stage by reminding students that Brainstorm means writing down all of your ideas without stopping to think about which ones will work.
- Give each student a blank sheet of paper. Instruct them to work alone to brainstorm ideas for a waterproof sandwich container made of the materials they've just investigated.
- Allow 10 minutes for students to work. As they do, walk around the room and look over their shoulders. Ask questions that guide students to think of new possibilities. Suggested questions:

  Which materials could keep the sandwich dry? Which ones could help float the sandwich? Why do you think that?

  Which material are you using here? Why did you choose that material?

  What job does this material do? Are any other materials good for that job?

  Is there another way to make the container float? To make it open and close? To make it waterproof?

- At the end of Brainstorm, ask students to choose one idea they like best and circle it.

3 ▶ Plan
30 minutes

- Instruct students to form groups of four (or three as needed). Stand back and let students form groups independently, in whatever way they choose. Students should sit down once they've formed their groups.
- After groups have formed, students need to choose jobs (descriptions on page 7). They may choose jobs in any manner as long as each person has at least one job and all four jobs are assigned.
- Give each person in the group a new blank sheet of paper. Tell them that each group member will draw a copy of the group plan, and that all plans within a group need to match. This shows that each person understands the plan in the same way. All plans need to be labeled.
- Set the timer for 20 minutes. Remind students to take turns sharing ideas from Brainstorm before deciding on anything for the group plan.
- Visit with each group as they work. Compliment good collaborative behaviors. Challenge students to think outside of the box and to stretch their thinking as they use everything they know about how materials react in water. Suggested questions:

  How will the sandwich go in and out of the container?

  How did you work together to create this plan?

  What part of this design will make the sandwich float?

Build
40 minutes

- Tell students it is time to build the waterproof sandwich containers.
- As a class, review the procedure for building. Call on student volunteers to list the steps in order, one at a time.
  - Follow the plan as you build.
  - Change the plan only if there is a good engineering reason to do so (for example, the plan isn't working as expected).
  - Notify the teacher and explain the reason for any change.
  - Make changes to the original plan in a new color, or draw up a new one and label it Plan 2.
- Invite the Materials Managers to pick up materials kits. Set the timer for 30 minutes.
- Move around the room, checking on students' work. Push students to be innovative without making direct suggestions. Ask questions that force students to rely on their observations and to explain their thinking. Sample questions:

  What else do you know about sinking, floating, and what happens when materials are placed in water? How do you know these things?

  How did your observations in Investigate help you design this container?

  How do you know if it works? Will you test ahead of time?

  How did you divide the work for this project?
- Allow students to test their containers in water during Build.
- Place the completed sandwich containers in a safe place until it is time to test.

Test & Present
5–10 minutes per group to test; 2–3 minutes per group to present

- Set up a tub full of water to use for testing. Give each Recorder a Product Score sheet. Have the timer available.
- Call the first group up to test their waterproof container. Ask the Speaker to describe how they designed and built the container. Let students in the other groups ask questions.
- Instruct the Materials Manager to place the sandwich inside the container, seal it, and then place the container in the water. The Timekeeper sets the timer for 1 minute.
- After 1 minute, the Recorder writes down scores for items 1 to 4 on the Product Score sheet. Next, ask the Materials Manager to open the container. Let three students from another group judge the dryness of the sandwich and give it a score based on the Product Score sheet.
- If the sandwich was dry, the materials manager places it back into the container, seals it, then places the container back in the water. This time the sandwich stays in for 2 minutes before checking. Continue this procedure until the sandwich is wet or until it has stayed dry for 5 minutes. (An alternative approach is to return the sandwich container to the water for additional 1-minute intervals, rather than increasing the time of each test.)

- After each group has tested their container, remind Recorders to tally up the final score.
- Give each group an opportunity to present their results. After all groups have had a chance to present, ask the following questions and allow time for class discussion:

  Which container had the highest score?

  Do you agree that the container with the highest score is "the best" container? Why or why not?

  Which of the five scoring items do you think is most important? Did "the best" container do well on that scoring item?

  Do you think people might have different ideas about which product is "the best," based on what they think is important?

- Provide a copy of the Checklist for each student.

Opportunities for Differentiation

To make it simpler: Demonstrate some techniques to the class that will help to make something float. Show how to fold the aluminum foil and to fill a baggy with air to make it buoyant. Provide two plastic or plastic foam plates instead of paper plates.

To make it harder: Make the cargo heavier by adding ingredients to the sandwich or by including a few baby carrots.

Names _____

_____

_____

_____

Waterproof Container Product Score

Criteria: Score 0, 1, 2, or 3 for items 1 to 4.	Score
❶ Fit of sandwich	_____
❷ Ease of use	_____
❸ Durability	_____
❹ Flotation	_____
❺ Waterproof Score 1 point for each minute the sandwich stays dry, from 0 to 5 points	_____
Total score	_____

Name _____

Waterproof Container Checklist

❶ I had this group job. Circle one:

Recorder   Timekeeper

Speaker   Materials Manager

One way I did my group job was:

_____

_____

On a scale of 1 to 5, rate your group as a whole.
1 is low. 5 is high.

❷ Working together: _____

❸ Use of time: _____

❹ Use of materials: _____

Appendices

References

Barell, John. 2006. *Problem Based Learning: An Inquiry Approach*. Thousand Oaks, CA: Corwin Press.

Boaler, Jo. 1998. "Open and Closed Mathematics: Student Experiences and Understandings." *Journal for Research in American Mathematics Education,* 29 (1), 41.

Bransford, John D., Ann L. Brown, and Rodney R. Cocking, ed. 2000. *How People Learn: Brain, Mind, Experience, and School: Expanded Edition*. Washington, D.C.: National Academies Press.

Drew, David E. 2011. *STEM the Tide: Reforming Science, Technology, Engineering, and Math Education in America*. Baltimore, MD: The Johns Hopkins University Press.

Helm, Judy Harris, and Lillian Katz. 2001. *Young Investigators: The Project Approach in the Early Years*. New York: Teachers College Press.

Jacobs, Heidi Hayes. 2010. *Curriculum 21: Essential Education for a Changing World*. Alexandria, VA: Association for Supervision and Curriculum Development.

Lantz, Hayes Blaine, Jr. 2009. "STEM Education: What Form? What Function?" *SEEN* Magazine 11 (2): 28-29.

Larmer, John, and John R. Mergendoller, 2010. "7 Essentials for Project-Based Learning." *Educational Leadership* 68 (1).

MacDonell, Colleen. 2006. *Project-Based Inquiry Units for Young Children: First Steps to Research for Grades Pre-K–2*. Santa Barbara, CA: Linworth Libraries Limited.

Nagel, Nancy G. 1996. *Learning Through Real World Problem Solving: The Power of Integrative Teaching*. Thousand Oaks, CA: Corwin Press.

Schunn, Christian D. 2009. "How Kids Learn Engineering: The Cognitive Science Perspective." *The Bridge: Linking Engineering and Society* 39 (3): 32-37.

Wiggins, Grant, and Jay McTighe. 2005. *Understanding by Design, 2nd ed.* Alexandria, VA: Association for Supervision and Curriculum Development.

Organizations & Initiatives

American Society for Engineering Education (ASEE)
eGFI (Engineering—Go For It!)
1818 N Street NW, Suite 600
Washington, DC 20036
www.egfi-k12.org

ASCD (formerly Association for Supervision and Curriculum Development)
1703 N. Beauregard Street
Alexandria, VA 22311-1714
www.ascd.org

The Coalition for Science After School
University of California
Lawrence Hall of Science, #5200
Berkeley, CA 94720-5200
www.afterschoolscience.org

Common Core State Standards Initiative
www.corestandards.org

International Society for Technology in Education
1710 Rhode Island Avenue NW, Suite 900
Washington, DC 20036
www.iste.org

International Technology and Engineering Educators Association
1914 Association Drive, Suite 201
Reston, VA 20191-1539
www.iteea.org

Next Generation Science Standards
Achieve, Inc.
1400 16th Street NW, Suite 510
Washington, DC 20036
www.nextgenscience.org

The Partnership for 21st Century Skills
1 Massachusetts Avenue NW, Suite 700
Washington, DC 20001
www.p21.org

Teach Engineering: Resources for K–12
www.teachengineering.org

Content & Skills Alignment Charts

Common Core Standards for Mathematical Practice	Engineering Challenges																			
	Apple Containers	Nut Sorters	Columbus Day Sailboats	Pumpkin Packages	Native American Style Drums	Thanksgiving Snack Assembly Lines	Candy Houses	Candle Holders	New Year's Noisemakers	Snowman Huts	Groundhog Shadow Hiders	Valentine Mailboxes	Kites	Butterfly Habitats	April Shower Umbrellas	Nests	May Flower Watering Systems	Farm Fences	Fish Catchers	Waterproof Containers
1. Make sense of problems and persevere in solving them.	X	X	X	X	X	X	X	X	X	X	X	X	X	X	X	X	X	X	X	X
2. Reason abstractly and quantitatively.	X	X	X	X	X	X	X	X	X	X	X	X	X	X	X	X	X	X	X	X
3. Construct viable arguments and critique the reasoning of others.	X	X	X	X	X	X	X	X	X	X	X	X	X	X	X	X	X	X	X	X
4. Model with mathematics.	X	X	X	X	X	X	X	X	X	X	X	X	X	X	X	X	X	X	X	X
5. Use appropriate tools strategically.	X	X	X	X	X	X	X	X	X	X	X	X	X	X	X	X	X	X	X	X
6. Attend to precision.	X	X	X	X	X	X	X	X	X	X	X	X	X	X	X	X	X	X	X	X
7. Look for and make use of structure.	X	X	X	X	X	X	X	X	X	X	X	X	X	X	X	X	X	X	X	X
8. Look for and express regularity in repeated reasoning.	X			X			X	X	X	X			X					X	X	

A Framework for K–12 Science Education	Engineering Challenges																			
	Apple Containers	Nut Sorters	Columbus Day Sailboats	Pumpkin Packages	Native American Style Drums	Thanksgiving Snack Assembly Lines	Candy Houses	Candle Holders	New Year's Noisemakers	Snowman Huts	Groundhog Shadow Hiders	Valentine Mailboxes	Kites	Butterfly Habitats	April Shower Umbrellas	Nests	May Flower Watering Systems	Farm Fences	Fish Catchers	Waterproof Containers
PS2.C: Whether an object stays still or moves often depends on the effects of multiple pushes and pulls on it.	X	X	X	X									X	X	X		X	X	X	X
PS3.B: Sunlight warms Earth's surface.									X	X										
PS3.C: A bigger push or pull makes things go faster. Faster speeds during a collision can cause a bigger change in shape of the colliding objects.			X										X			X		X		
PS4.A: Waves . . . can be made in water by disturbing the surface.			X																	X
PS4.A: Sound can make matter vibrate, and vibrating matter can make sound.					X															
PS4.B: Objects can be seen only when light is available to illuminate them.								X		X										
PS4C: People use their senses to learn about the world around them.	X	X	X	X	X	X	X	X	X	X	X	X	X	X	X	X	X	X	X	X
PS4.C: People . . . use a variety of devices to communicate . . . over long distances.					X															
LS1.B: Plants and animals grow and change.				X		X								X			X	X	X	
LS1.C: All animals need food in order to live and grow . . . . Plants need water and light to live and grow.				X		X								X			X		X	
LS2.A: Animals depend on their surroundings to get what they need, including food, water, shelter, and a favorable temperature.							X	X						X		X			X	
LS2.B: Organisms obtain the materials they need to grow and survive from the environment.	X			X										X			X	X	X	
LS4.C: Living things can survive only where their needs are met.				X		X								X			X		X	

A Framework for K–12 Science Education	Apple Containers	Nut Sorters	Columbus Day Sailboats	Pumpkin Packages	Native American Style Drums	Thanksgiving Snack Assembly Lines	Candy Houses	Candle Holders	New Year's Noisemakers	Snowman Huts	Groundhog Shadow Hiders	Valentine Mailboxes	Kites	Butterfly Habitats	April Shower Umbrellas	Nests	May Flower Watering Systems	Farm Fences	Fish Catchers	Waterproof Containers
ESS2.D: Weather is the combination of sunlight, wind, snow or rain, and temperature in a particular region at a particular time.										X	X		X		X					
ESS3.C: Things that people do to live comfortably can affect the world around them.							X									X	X		X	
ETS1.A: Asking questions, making observations, and gathering information are helpful in thinking about [engineering] problems. Before beginning to design a solution, it is important to clearly understand the problem.	X	X	X	X	X	X	X	X	X	X	X	X	X	X	X	X	X	X	X	X
ETS1.B: Designs can be conveyed through sketches, drawings, or physical models.	X	X	X	X	X	X	X	X	X	X	X	X	X	X	X	X	X	X	X	X
ETS1.B: To design something complicated, one may need to break the problem into parts and attend to each part separately but must then bring the parts together to test the overall plan.	X	X	X	X	X	X	X	X	X	X	X	X	X	X	X	X	X	X	X	X
ETS1.C: Because there is always more than one possible solution to a problem, it is useful to compare designs, test them, and discuss their strengths and weaknesses.	X	X	X	X	X	X	X	X	X	X	X	X	X	X	X	X	X	X	X	X
ETS2.A: There are many types of tools produced by engineering that can be used in science to help answer . . . questions through observation or measurement. Observations and measurements are also used in engineering to help test and refine design ideas.	X	X	X	X	X	X	X	X	X	X	X	X	X	X	X	X	X	X	X	X
ETS2.B: People depend on various technologies in their lives; human life would be very different without technology.	X	X	X	X	X	X	X	X	X	X	X	X	X	X	X	X	X	X	X	X
ETS2.B: Every human-made product is designed by applying some knowledge of the natural world and is built by using materials derived from the natural world.	X	X	X	X	X	X	X	X	X	X	X	X	X	X	X	X	X	X	X	X

21st Century Learning Core Subjects and Student Outcomes	Engineering Challenges																			
	Apple Containers	Nut Sorters	Columbus Day Sailboats	Pumpkin Packages	Native American Style Drums	Thanksgiving Snack Assembly Lines	Candy Houses	Candle Holders	New Year's Noisemakers	Snowman Huts	Groundhog Shadow Hiders	Valentine Mailboxes	Kites	Butterfly Habitats	April Shower Umbrellas	Nests	May Flower Watering Systems	Farm Fences	Fish Catchers	Waterproof Containers
ELA			X		X		X		X	X	X				X			X		
Science			X	X	X	X			X	X	X	X	X	X	X	X	X		X	X
Math	X	X		X		X	X	X	X	X		X	X	X		X	X	X		
Arts					X	X	X	X	X		X		X		X					
Creativity and innovation	X	X	X	X	X	X	X	X	X	X	X	X	X	X	X	X	X	X	X	X
Critical thinking and problem solving	X	X	X	X	X	X	X	X	X	X	X	X	X	X	X	X	X	X	X	X
Communication and collaboration	X	X	X	X	X	X	X	X	X	X	X	X	X	X	X	X	X	X	X	X
Information and communications technology literacy			X	X	X						X	X			X	X		X		
Flexibility and adaptability	X	X	X	X	X	X	X	X	X	X	X	X	X	X	X	X	X	X	X	X
Initiative and self-direction	X	X	X	X	X	X	X	X	X	X	X	X	X	X	X	X	X	X	X	X
Social and cross-cultural skills	X	X	X	X	X	X	X	X	X	X	X	X	X	X	X	X	X	X	X	X
Productivity and accountability	X	X	X	X	X	X	X	X	X	X	X	X	X	X	X	X	X	X	X	X
Leadership and responsibility	X	X	X	X	X	X	X	X	X	X	X	X	X	X	X	X	X	X	X	X

You Might Also Be Interested in These Other Products from Crystal Springs Books

I Am an Engineer! Stickers
Every good engineer deserves to be rewarded. As your students meet the challenges in this book, acknowledge their accomplishments with these colorful 1½-in. stickers. Students love earning them — not to mention showing off their success to parents and peers alike!
(K–2) 48 stickers #A10785

Accidental Techie to the Rescue!
Simple Tech Solutions for Your Biggest Classroom Challenges
Lori Elliott, EdD, "The Accidental Techie"
"Accidental Techie" and former teacher Lori Elliott has researched loads of great websites so you don't have to. You'll learn how to use technology to engage students, build collaboration skills, interact with classrooms around the globe, and more. With Lori as your guide and technology as a tool, you and your students will reach new heights of enthusiasm and learning.
(K–6) 224 pp. #550227

Teach Like a Techie
20 Tools for Reaching the Digital Generation
Lori Elliott, EdD, "The Accidental Techie"
You can meet the digital natives on their own turf with this step-by-step guide to educational technology. Podcasts? Prezi? SMART Boards? Blogs? No problem, with the "Accidental Techie" as your guide. Lori focuses not on bells and whistles but on simple applications that can immediately bring new relevance, energy, and enthusiasm to your classroom.
(K–12) 192 pp. #550209

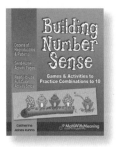

Building Number Sense
Games & Activities to Practice Combinations to 10
Catherine Jones Kuhns
Make number-fact practice fresh and fun all year long! As students enjoy activities that require them to take off their shoes, toss coins, and oink like pigs, they'll be engaged in the critical practice they need to truly master those all-important number combinations to 10. Reproducibles and patterns make these strategies a snap to implement, and your students will love practicing number bonds with the 8 pages of full-color pull-out strips!
(K–1) 72 pp. #402659

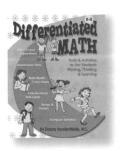

Differentiated Math
Tools & Activities to Get Students Moving, Thinking & Learning
Donna VanderWeide
Donna has packed this book with songs, rhymes, games, "investigations," and so much more—all designed to bring the power of differentiation to your math instruction. She offers a "training camp" for graphs and glyphs; task cards to give students choices; and loads of reproducibles to simplify preparation, planning, and assessment. Math class has never been more exciting!
(K–3) 192 pp. #454898